Halloween Traditions in Boston

ANTHONY M. SAMMARCO

AMERICA THROUGH TIME®
ADDING COLOR TO AMERICAN HISTORY

This book is dedicated to Stingy Jack with the hope that his eternal earthly wanderings have not been in vain.

America Through Time is an imprint of Fonthill Media LLC
www.through-time.com
office@through-time.com

Published by Arcadia Publishing by arrangement with Fonthill Media LLC
For all general information, please contact Arcadia Publishing:
Telephone: 843-853-2070
Fax: 843-853-0044
E-mail: sales@arcadiapublishing.com
For customer service and orders:
Toll-Free 1-888-313-2665

www.arcadiapublishing.com

First published 2022

ISBN 978-1-63499-413-2

Typeset in Mrs Eaves XL Serif Narrow
Printed and bound in England

Contents

Acknowledgments

I wish to extend my sincere thanks and deep appreciation to:

Joel Andreasen; Carl Bertolino, of Jack's Joke Shop in Boston; Boston Public Library, David Leonard; British Library, London; Pasqualina and Donato Cedmarco; Cesidio "Joe" Cedrone; Edie Clifford; Colortek, Jackie Anderson; the late Rupert A.M. Davis; Robin Dexter; Digital Commonwealth; eBay; Mary Ann English; J. Paul Getty Museum, Los Angeles; Edward Gordon; Helen Hannon; Harvard University Art Museum; Thomas and Nancy High; George Kalchev, Fonthill Media; Peter B. Kingman; Kena Longabaugh; Maine State Library, Sarah Stanton; the late Martin Manning; Mary Ann Sammartino Nagle; the late Frank Norton; Orleans Camera; Peabody Essex Museum; Phillips Chocolates, Joseph Sammartino, Jr., Philip Strazzula III and Matthew Sammartino; Lilian M.C. Randall; Henry Scannell; Ron Scully; Alan Sutton, Fonthill Media; Jamie Sutton; Archives and Special Collections, University of Massachusetts, Sammarco Collection; Kenneth Turino and Chris Matthias; Worcester Historical Museum.

Introduction

Noah Webster describes Halloween as "October 31: observed especially with dressing up in disguise, trick-or-treating, and displaying jack o'lanterns during the evening." However, Halloween is more than simply a date or dressing up in disguise; it has deep roots in the Celtic culture of Scotland, Ireland, Wales, Cornwall, Brittany, and the Isle of Man. Halloween is short for All Hallows' Eve and has its origins dating back to the ancient Celtic festival of Samhain, the Celtic New Year's festival. The Mórrígan was the Celtic deity associated with war and fate who led her people, often appearing as a crow. All Hallows really means "summer's end," and the festival celebrated the end of the harvest season and the coming of winter. The Celts believed that the veil between the worlds of the living and the dead were thinnest at this time, and the dead could return and walk where they once had before. Further, those who had died in the past year and who, for one reason or another, had not yet moved on, would do so at this time and could interact with the living.

However, by the fifth century, Christianity had come to Ireland and the pagan rituals were eventually Christianized. Pagan symbols, temples, festivals, the legends, including the Samhain festival, as well as many others, were transformed. In fact, the Samhain festival had long been associated with all those who had gone on before, with the earth, the change of the year, and this transformation marked by celebration. Once the festival was Christianized, All Hallows' Eve evolved into a night of vigil, prayer, and fasting in preparation for the next day when the saints were honored at a far tamer celebration.

When the Puritans arrived in Boston in 1630, they brought with them from England these traditions, but they refused to observe any holidays which might be associated with pagan beliefs, including Christmas, Easter, and Halloween. However, Pope's Night in Boston had evolved from an English celebration called Guy Fawkes Day. This holiday commemorated the discovery of the Gunpowder Plot, an attempt by Guy Fawkes to assassinate King James I and replace him with a Catholic monarch. With extravagant effigies, which often consisted of comical images of the Pope and the Devil, residents of the North End and the South End, along with droves of children parading through the streets with miniature versions of the effigies, had massive parades of these two effigies. When the two parades collided, they would fight to try to seize the other's effigy. If the

North End won this fight, the effigies would be dragged to Copp's Hill and burned; if the South End won, Boston Common was the effigies' final resting place. During the Revolution, General George Washington banned the effigy parades. It would be in the mid-nineteenth century, with the immigration of the Irish to Boston during the potato famine, and Scots from Scotland, that the first vestiges of what evolved as Halloween began to appear. The Irish, largely Roman Catholic, continued to observe All Hallows' Eve, All Saint's Day, and All Soul's Day along with the practice of "souling," but these festivals were still infused with age old folk traditions such as the jack o'lantern.

The jack o'lantern is associated with the Irish folk tale of Stingy Jack, a clever con man who fooled the devil into banning him from hell, but because of his sinful life, could not enter heaven. After his death, he roamed the world carrying a small lantern made from a turnip with a red-hot ember from hell inside to light his way. Many believe this legend evolved from sightings of will-o-the-wisp, swamp and marsh gasses which glowed in the night. On All Hallows' Eve, the Irish hollowed out turnips and carved them with faces, placing a candle inside, so that as they went about "souling" on the night when the veil between life and death was thinnest, they would be protected from spirits like Stingy Jack.

The basics of Halloween in Boston were now in place, thanks to the immigrants in the nineteenth century from Ireland and the British Isles, with children going from house to house asking for sweet treats in the form of soul cakes and carrying jack o'lanterns. Shortly after their arrival in the United States, the Irish had substituted the turnip for the pumpkin as their lantern of choice on Halloween as it was much easier to carve. The term trick-or-treating had evolved, as it meant young people and children went on a destructive bend if they were not given treats, such as soul cakes and later candy.

A Witch's Lament

Oh, yes of course, it's all our fault!
The milk is sour, the sugar's salt!
The gate is stolen from the fence
It's up a pole full twelve blocks hence!
A rope is stretched across the walk
Of course! Just go ahead and talk
All of the tricks that you have seen
You lay to us on Hallowe'en!

To try and eliminate the widespread property destruction by the revelers, communities began to hold Halloween festivities that might include a band, costume contests, and a parade that redirected the night into one of a celebration. Now people of all ages began to enjoy a festive, rather than disruptive, Halloween.

A lot of people think of Halloween as a truly American holiday. In some ways it really is a very American holiday, because over the decades it has grown to enormous proportions.

However, people don't remember that its roots are Celtic. Americans began to dress up in costumes and go house to house asking for food or money, a practice that eventually became today's "trick-or-treat" tradition. At the turn of the century, Halloween parties for both children and adults became the most common way to celebrate the day, with apple bobbing, often with a coin inserted in the apple, and pie eating contests. Parties focused on games, foods of the season, and festive costumes. By the 1920s and 1930s, Halloween had become a secular, community-centered holiday, with parades and town-wide Halloween parties as the featured entertainment.

On Halloween, when it was believed that ghosts came back to the earthly world, people thought that they would encounter ghosts if they left their homes. To avoid being recognized by these ghosts, people would wear masks when they left their homes after dark so that the ghosts would mistake them for fellow spirits. By the turn of the twentieth century, masks had given way to costumes, and companies such as Weldon's produced catalogs of fancy dress for Halloween as well as Collegeville Costumes in the mid-twentieth century with popular comic book and television characters. With costumes, party decorations and articles on how to make things at home, the celebration of Halloween began to rival major holidays.

Today, Halloween seems to be a night when children roam the streets dressed in costumes and masks, or homemade attire, and seek candy from every house within walking distance. Candy companies such as Curtiss, Brachs, Nestlé, Schrafft's, Mars, Hershey, Luden's, Carlton's, and Necco among others offered everything under the sun, from the well-known Baby Ruth, Butterfinger, Mars Bar, 5th Avenue, Nestlé Crunch, and Nut Log candy bars to Cracker Jack, Wrigley's Chewing gum, WOWE-E Chewing Gum Whistles, PEZ Candy, Indian Corn, and even fresh fruit. One could send family and friends greetings on Halloween, and early manufacturers of Halloween cards were George Whitney Company, Gibson Card, Hallmark Cards, and Rustcraft Cards, who produced both cards and postcards to send that were drawn and illustrated by such notable artists as Norman Rockewell, Tasha Tudor, Ellen Clapsaddle, Frances Brundage, and many others who caught the spirit of the holiday in jack o'lanterns, ghosts, witches, black cats, and dancing skeletons that illustrated not only their card designs but were popular choices for Halloween costumes.

In *Halloween Traditions in Boston*, the history of the Salem Witchcraft Trials is discussed, which caused such tremendous anxiety and fear and the deaths of many innocent people in Massachusetts Bay Colony in 1692. The decorating of Beacon Hill as a veritable neighborhood of whimsy with macabre skulls, bones, and cobwebs, to pumpkins and lighted jack o'lanterns, is also discussed. Trick-or-treating in the twentieth century, with children dressing as favorite characters from both comic books as well as television and cartoons, was an exciting night to look forward to. With plastic pumpkin buckets or large paper bags to collect candy, the excitement was not just in the door to door collecting of treats but returning home afterwards to inspect the loot. Often there was a month's load of candy that had been collected, and though the now excited child was allowed a few pieces before bedtime, it was more often than not a treat in school lunch boxes for the next few weeks.

Halloween might be an old-fashioned way of saying "the night before All Saints' Day," but it has become so much more than that. Halloween is still considered a powerful turning point in the wheel of the year, signifying the cycle of life, death, and rebirth. The pumpkin is often linked to rebirth and fertility and symbolizes harvests and crops. So, with a tip of the hat to the ancient Celtic festival of Samhain, we realize that Halloween has come full circle.

Since this is the time for goblins and bats,
Halloween spirits, ghosts and cats,
Weird-happenings and witches brew,
These are the things I wish for you.

This postcard of a young boy reading *Ghost Stories* by author Hal Loween can lead to a Bewitching Halloween! Obviously frightened by the stories in the book, the young boy glances out the window, and seen in the light of a full moon there is a ghost, a bat, and two equally frightened boys staring back at him.

1

Witchcraft and the Salem Trials

This dramatic painting is titled *The Examination of a Witch* and was painted by Thompkins H. Matteson in 1853. The painting depicts Mary Fisher, a young girl accused of being a witch during the Salem Witchcraft Trials, who was seized by Deputy Governor Richard Bellingham in the absence of Governor John Endicott, and shamefully stripped to the waist for the purpose of ascertaining whether or not she was indeed a witch and whether or not there was a Devil's mark upon her. The mark of the Devil could be anything from bruises or blemishes to moles or marks, but it was the uncontrolled hysteria that the Devil had descended upon Salem that caused a town-wide panic. (Collection Peabody Essex Museum)

A page from *The Hours of René d'Anjou,* printed in 1410, is a grim reminder of the dead on All Hallows' Eve and the fact that they were once as we are today. René, Duke of Anjou, and King of Naples had this gruesome portrait placed at the beginning of the *Office of the Dead,* depicting him as a decomposing corpse holding a banner that reads, *Memento homo quod sinis es et in sinere reverteris* (Remember that you are dust and to dust you will return.) Not only is this illuminated manuscript macabre, with a corpse's grimacing face and deeply penetrating eye sockets, but it faces us in a passage from life to death, reminding one of their own mortality. The depiction, of a corpse wearing a gold *fleur de lis* tipped crown, clutching a scroll that unfolds, reminds the readers that one day, they too will return to dust. The illustration reminds one to be ever devout in their faith, and do good deeds, because one day all will be judged. (Collection The British Library)

Denise Poncher before a Vision of Death, from the Poncher Hours, was depicted by the Master of the Chronique Scandaleuse about 1500 in Paris. All Hallows' Eve was an important part of the Church calendar in the Middle Ages and was a night to commemorate the dead, to repent, to fast, and to prepare oneself for All Hallows' Day on November 1. This church feast honored all saints, both known and forgotten, and celebrated the end of the summer harvest and the coming of winter. This illustration is a page from *The Office of the Dead,* a Catholic prayer book that was commissioned for Denise Poncher, probably on the occasion of her marriage. Dressed in a red gown, she is on her knees before a particularly macabre representation of Death, which is carrying four scythes and has already claimed three people. Death is standing over dead bodies and is coming for Denise. Despite the rotting flesh sloughing off and the maggots writhing in and out of him, Denise is not scared, and her luminous white skin contrasts with Death's grisly decomposition. She kneels with her prayer book in hand, soul shriven and ready for Heaven. (Collection The J. Paul Getty Museum)

A MOST
Certain, Strange, and true Discovery of a
VVITCH.
Being taken by some of the Parliament Forces, as she was standing on a small planck-board and sayling on it over the River of Newbury:
Together with the strange and true manner of her death, with the propheticall words and speeches she used at the same time.

Printed by John Hammond, 1643.

A Most Certain, Strange, and True Discovery of a Witch was printed by John Hammond in London in 1643. The pamphlet was written during the English Civil War and describes the "Witch of Newbury, England" as a "*tall, lean, slender woman, as [a soldier] supposed, to his amazement, and great terreur treading of the water with her feet, with as much ease and firmnesse as if one should walk or trample on the earth.*" Overtaken by the Parliament Forces, the purported witch was fired upon by the soldiers and "with a deriding and loud laughter ... she caught their bullets in her hands and chew'd them." Depicted as an old barefoot woman, she was further beset by two black ravens, the harbingers of doom and oft companions to witches. The pamphlet ends "*they immediately discharged a Pistoll underneath her eare, at which she straight sunk down and dyed, leaving her legacy of a detested carcasse to the wormes, her soul we ought not to judge of, though the evills of her wicked life and death can scape no censure.*"

A Modest Enquiry
Into the Nature of
Witchcraft,
AND
How Persons Guilty of that Crime may be *Convicted*: And the means used for their Discovery Discussed, both *Negatively* and *Affirmatively*, according to *SCRIPTURE* and *EXPERIENCE*.

By John Hale,
Pastor of the Church of Christ in *Beverley*,
Anno Domini 1697.

When they say unto you, seek unto them that have Familiar Spirits and unto Wizzards that peep, &c. To the Law and to the Testimony; if they speak not according to this word, it is because there is no light in them, Isaiah VIII. 19, 20.
That which I see not teach thou me, Job 34. 32.

BOSTON in N. E.
Printed by *B. Green*, and *J. Allen*, for *Benjamin Eliot* under the Town House: 1702

A Modest Enquiry Into the Nature of Witchcraft was written by Reverend John Hale, pastor of the Church of Christ in Beverly, Massachusetts, in 1697. Hale wrote about the infamous Salem Witch Trials, and in his incendiary writings he challenged the legal proceedings and religious principles of witch hunts in general, as his wife Sarah Noyes Hale was one of the many people who had been accused of being a witch. In fact, it was said that Hale suggested that the fear of witchcraft was so great that it impaired the minds and judgment of everyone involved in the Salem Witch Trials, possibly resulting in the death of innocent people.

And when they shall say unto you, Seek unto them that have familiar spirits, and unto wizards that peep, and that mutter: should not a people seek unto their God? for the living to the dead?

Isaiah 8: 19

The Reverend Increase Mather (1639–1723) was the son of Reverend Richard Mather, a staunch Puritan minister from Dorchester. Educated at Harvard College, Mather opposed anything openly contradictory to, mutually exclusive with, or potentially distracting from his Puritanical and narrow religious beliefs, taught by his father and the Puritan hierarchy. When Sir Edmund Andros came to Massachusetts as the governor of the Dominion of New England and restored the papist holidays and allowed a Maypole to be set up in Charlestown, Mather was shocked and appalled. In fact, he said that the Devil had "begun his march of triumph" in Boston. Mather served as the minister at Second Church in Boston from 1664 to 1723 and was involved with the government of the Massachusetts Bay Colony; he served as president of Harvard College from 1685 to 1702.

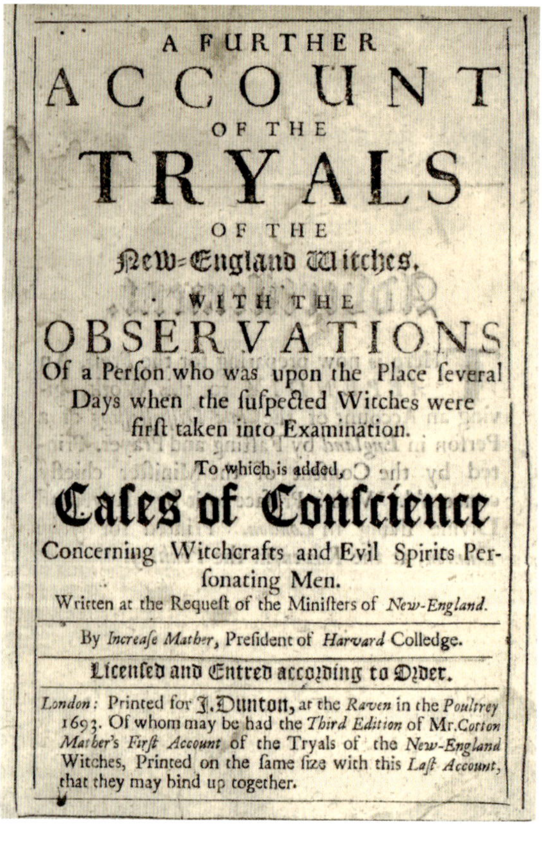

A FURTHER

ACCOUNT

OF THE

TRYALS

OF THE

New-England Witches.

WITH THE

OBSERVATIONS

Of a Perſon who was upon the Place ſeveral Days when the ſuſpected Witches were firſt taken into Examination.

To which is added,

Caſes of Conſcience

Concerning Witchcrafts and Evil Spirits Perſonating Men.

Written at the Requeſt of the Miniſters of *New-England.*

By *Increaſe Mather*, Preſident of *Harvard* Colledge.

Licenſed and Entred according to Order.

London: Printed for J. Dunton, at the *Raven* in the *Poultrey* 1693. Of whom may be had the *Third Edition* of Mr. *Cotton Mather's Firſt Account* of the Tryals of the *New-England* Witches, Printed on the ſame ſize with this *Laſt Account*, that they may bind up together.

A Further Account of the Tryals of the New England Witches was written by Increase Mather at the request of the ministers of New England and printed by John Dunton in London in 1693. As Mather was president of Harvard College and a respected clergyman, the book outlined the observations of a person who was upon the place several days when the suspected witches were first taken into examination. In his book he called into question the use of "spectral" and other evidences allowed to be used by the judges in the witch trials. In the *Cases of Conscience,* it states: "Doubts arose, as we have stated [about evidence used in the trials], and it came about that the subject of the witch trials was discussed by the ministers on August the first [1692]." Their conclusions, unanimous but as yet vague and indecisive, were expressed in these words: "*That the Devil may sometimes have a Permission to Represent an Innocent Person as tormenting such as are under Diabolical Molestations. But such things are rare and extraordinary, especially when such Matters come before Civil Judicatures.*"

The Reverend Cotton Mather was the son of Increase Mather and grandson of the two foremost Puritan ministers in New England, Richard Mather and John Cotton. A graduate of Harvard College, he was a socially and politically influential Puritan minister at the Second Church in Boston from 1685 to 1728, and a prolific author, having written 450 books and pamphlets. His ubiquitous literary works made him one of the most influential religious leaders in America. However, his narrow mindedness was evident when Reverend George Burroughs recited a perfect rendition of the *Lord's Prayer* while on the Salem gallows, something Mather himself thought impossible for anyone guilty of an alliance with the Devil. The crowd was so moved that some wanted to prevent the execution. However, Mather proclaimed that Burroughs was no ordained minister, and that the "Devil has often been transformed into an Angel of Light." With those damning words, under the tearful gaze of an ambivalent crowd, George Burroughs was hanged.

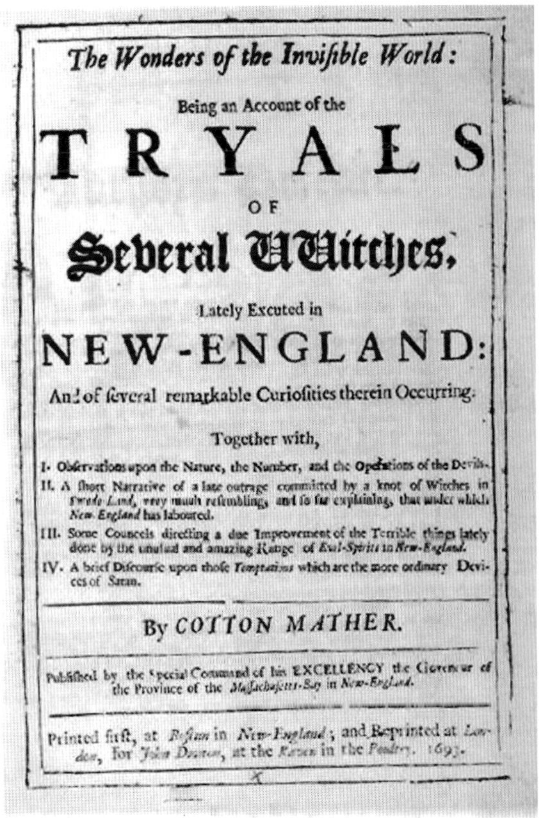

The Wonders of the Invisible World:

Being an Account of the

TRYALS

OF

Several Witches,

Lately Excuted in

NEW-ENGLAND:

And of several remarkable Curiosities therein Occurring.

Together with,

I. Observations upon the Nature, the Number, and the Operations of the Devils.

II. A short Narrative of a late outrage committed by a knot of Witches in Swede-Land, very much resembling, and so far explaining, that under which New-England has laboured.

III. Some Councels directing a due Improvement of the Terrible things lately done by the unusual and amazing Range of Evil-Spirits in New-England.

IV. A brief Discourse upon those Temptations which are the more ordinary Devices of Satan.

By COTTON MATHER.

Published by the Special Command of his EXCELLENCY the Governour of the Province of the Massachusetts-Bay in New-England.

Printed first, at Boston in New-England; and Reprinted at London, for John Dunton, at the Raven in the Poultry. 1693.

The Wonders of the Invisible World: Being an account of the Tryals of Several Witches lately executed in New England was written by Cotton Mather and printed in 1693 after the hysteria in Salem had subsided. Mather strongly defended the witchcraft trials in this account, depicting New England as a battleground where the forces of God and the forces of the Devil ultimately clashed. As a believer in the witchcraft that had possessed Salem in 1692, Mather wrote this book to not only outline the testimony from the many victims, but also to support his friends in the provincial government who had been involved in the trials. He gives detailed descriptions of each case, and created an invaluable record of the witchcraft trials, depicting New England as a battleground where the forces of good and evil clashed and caused turmoil.

Lieutenant Governor William Stoughton was appointed Chief Justice of the court of Oyer and Terminer in 1692. He ruled over the trials with the determination to eradicate all witches from Massachusetts Bay Colony and he was heavily influenced by his conservative and narrow-minded Puritan convictions. It was he who allowed spectral evidence of the afflicted girls to accuse their fellow townspeople of witchcraft. When the court was dissolved, Stoughton continued to enjoy political success and never apologized for his role in the trials. In the Court of Oyer and Terminer, the Chief Magistrate was William Stoughton, and the other judges were John Richards, Nathaniel Saltonstall, who resigned from the court over the nature of the proceedings, Waitstill Winthrop, Bartholomew Gedney, Samuel Sewall, John Hathorne, Joanathan Corwin, and Peter Sergeant. (Collection of Harvard University Art Museum)

Samuel Sewall (1652–1730,) depicted as a judge in the Province of Massachusetts Bay by artist John Smibert, was best known for his involvement in the Salem witch trials for which he was one of three judges who sentenced people to death, but would later recant his actions and apologize. In 1681, he was appointed the official printer of the colony, and among the first works he published was John Bunyan's *The Pilgrim's Progress*. He served for many years as the chief justice of the Massachusetts Superior Court of Judicature, the province's high court. Sewall, brother of Court Clerk Stephen Sewall, was one of the nine judges who sentenced people to death in the Salem Witch Trials. (Collection Museum of Fine Arts, Boston)

The mass hysteria, turmoil, theatrical trials, and denunciations that led to the execution of twenty-one innocent people make the Salem Witch Trials one of the black marks against the Province of Massachusetts Bay Colony. This painting, *The Trial of George Jacobs for Witchcraft*, clearly shows the raw emotions of those in the room, but in the center is Jacobs' own granddaughter, who is pointing at him, accusing him of witchcraft. One of the judges rises from his chair as people react to the accusation. Jacobs was a prosperous farmer and well respected in Salem, and though he denied the allegation, he said "I am as innocent as a child born tonight." Jacobs was nonetheless found guilty and hanged as a witch on August 19, 1692. (Collection Peabody Essex Museum)

Salem Witch Trial is a colored lithograph by Charles Granger done in 1892 to commemorate the 200th anniversary of the trials at Salem. It depicts the raucous atmosphere of fear, trepidation, indignation, and raw emotion that ruled not just the judges of the Witch Trials, but those accused of witchcraft. Those executed in Salem were Sarah Good, Sarah Osborne, Bridget Bishop, Rebecca Nurse, Elizabeth Howe, Susannah Martin, Sarah Wildes, Reverend George Burroughs, George Jacobs, Martha Carrier, John Proctor, John Willard, Martha Corey, Mary Towne Easty, Mary Ayer Parker, Alice Parker, Ann Pudeator, Wilmot Redd, Margaret Scott, Samuel Wardwell, and Giles Corey, who was pressed to death. Those who died in prison were Ann Alcock Foster, Sarah Warren Osborn, and Roger Toothaker.

On June 2, the specially convened Court of Oyer and Terminer—"oyer" meaning "to hear" and "terminer" meaning "to decide"—sat for the first time and was presided over by Lieutenant Governor William Stoughton, who is seated at the bench. He was the newly appointed lieutenant governor of the Province of Massachusetts Bay. As chief justice, Stoughton believed that spectral evidence presented to the court, which constituted evidence gathered from dreams and visions, would form a central plank of the prosecutions. Two girls, held by guards, face their accusers, who are young girls wreathing, moaning, and pointing at the accused witches.

A colored lithograph of the *Trial of Giles Corey* by Charles Reinhart depicts a man—who was accused of witchcraft by Ann Putnam, Marcy Lewis, Abigail Williams, Mary Walcott, and Elizabeth Hubbard—being led into court. He pleaded "not guilty" but refused to be tried by the court which, in his view, had already determined his guilt, so he stood mute rather "putting himself on the country." He was sentenced to *peine forte et dure*, even though it was an illegal punishment, and ended up being tortuously crushed to death by heavy boulders on September 18, 1692. One of the major factors which made Giles Corey a prime target was not only his relationship with the rest of the community but also his past encounters with the law, including a prior conviction for murder. His chosen means of resistance and dramatic death reveal a strength of character.

2

All Hallows' Eve

Snap Apple Night, painted by the Irish painter Daniel Maclise, was celebrated on All Hallows' Eve, a time when supernatural influences prevail, the time when spirits, both the visible and invisible worlds, walk abroad and can be invoked by human powers for the purpose of revealing the mysterious future, and spirits may be called from the deep at will. The word "Hallowe'en" actually means "Saints" evening and it comes from a Scottish term for All Hallows' Eve, the evening before All Hallows' Day. Samhain, meaning summer's end, marked the harvest season and the beginning of winter or the "darker half" of the year and was celebrated with food, drink, dance, and revelry, as well as rituals and games intended to foretell one's future, especially regarding death and marriage.

There Peggy was dancing with Dan
While Maureen the lead was melting,
To prove how their fortunes ran
With the Cards could Nancy dealt in;
There was Kate, and her sweet-heart Will,
In nuts their true-love burning,
And poor Norah, though smiling still
She'd missed the snap-apple turning.

Halloween depicted in an etching by John Massey Wright of a painting by Edward Scriven that shows people around a brazier as an engaged girl places a nut on the fire. It was said that if the nuts burned quietly, the marriage would be happy; however, if the nut spat and hissed, the marriage would be stormy. However, if the girl put two nuts on the fire, one for her lover and one for herself, and the nuts spat and hissed, then this was obviously a bad omen for their future happiness.

Some merry friendly country folklore
Together did convene
To burn their nits [nuts,] an pou [pull] their stocks [plants]
An' haud [keep] their Halloween.

Robert Burns

Blindfolded by her family and friends, this girl stands before three bowls on the table as she plays the game of Three Luggies, which requires three bowls: one filled with clear water, one with milky water, and the last one empty. The three bowls are placed on the table and the young lady who wishes to play is blindfolded and led up to them.

She is then told to put her left hand into one of the bowls. If she dips her fingers in the clear water, she will marry a bachelor; if in the milky water, a widower; and if into the empty bowl, it is a sure sign that she will live in single blessedness all her days. This ceremony must be gone through with three times, and the hand be dipped twice in the same bowl, in order to make the prediction of any value.

A woman, striking a dramatic pose with a black lace shawl, wears a black gown sewn with crescents, stars, and snakes, and wears a tall brimless conical hat with crescents and stars, which uses the stars and moons as part of artistic license based on the supposed spirituality of a wizard and astrology connection. It's been said that the conical hat traditionally worn by wizards is symbolic of wisdom and intelligence, and that its pointed shape represents the cone of power, which is associated with the circle, the symbol of the sun, unity, eternity, rebirth, and the triangle.

A bejeweled woman in the late nineteenth century is dressed in an elaborate black gown, sewn with crescent moons and stars, as she holds a staff surmounted by a crescent moon from which a star is suspended. It has been said that witches of the Coven of the Crescent Moon "train with both blade and spell, and style themselves as the protectors of witchcraft, both within and without, and tend to be lawful in nature." Many who seek a Coven have pagan sensibilities of personal responsibility, pursuit of knowledge, tolerance, and live by the teachings of the Wiccan Rede.

Double, double toil and trouble;
Fire burn and cauldron bubble.
Fillet of a fenny snake,
In the cauldron boil and bake;
Eye of newt and toe of frog,
Wool of bat and tongue of dog,
Adder's fork and bling-worms sting,
Lizard's leg and howlet's wing,
For a charm of powerful trouble,
Like a hell-broth boil and bubble.

This young girl, dressed in an immaculate white lace dress with a star adorned witch's hat, holds a jack o'lantern. To complete the Halloween theme is a black cat sitting on a wicker chair and a smiling moon face hovering above.

There never was a Halloween nor any other day
With witches so be-witching as the charms which you display

These boys are dressed as an Indian and a clown for Halloween in 1905. Both hold jack o'lanterns that had a candle that when lit illuminated the dark as they roamed their neighborhoods looking for treats or pulling tricks. Halloween in early twentieth century was a night for pranks, tricks, and anarchy. Jack o'lanterns dangled from the ends of sticks, and teens jumped out from behind walls to terrorize smaller children. In fact, it was said that "Kids pulled fire alarms, threw bricks through shop windows, and painted obscenities on the principal's home. They struck out blindly against property owners, adults, and authority in general. They begged for money or sweets, and threatened vandalism if they didn't receive them."

This quartet of Halloween revelers in the late nineteenth century are dressed in black. Two are wearing witches' hats, with a stuffed owl on their laps as well as whisk brooms and a dust pan. There are plenty of superstitions concerning brooms, because the act of sweeping is inherently metaphorical.

When the owl and witch
together are seen
There's mischief brewing on
Halloween

The sign above this tableau reads "Shake hands with the ghost." With children bobbing for apples floating in a huge zinc tub, they hold their hands aloft as a friend dressed as a ghost hovers above them, and two levitate on either side. Bobbing for apples started in Europe hundreds of years ago as a common way for young lovers to court one another. If the bobber, typically a young girl, successfully bit into the apple with the name of a love interest in one go, then fortune favored the lucky couple and fate gave them the go-ahead. However, it is also said that first person to bite an apple would be the next one in the group to have a marriage.

A woman dressed as Annie Oakley poses for a photograph with two fellow Halloween revelers dressed as a prisoner in his striped uniform and the King of Spades. Oakley, whose real name was Phoebe Ann Mosey, was a crack sharpshooter who starred in Buffalo Bill's Wild West show. She joined Buffalo Bill in 1885, performing in Europe before royalty and other heads of state; she performed for Queen Victoria of the United Kingdom, King Umberto I of Italy, President Marie Francois Sadi Carnot of France, and other crowned heads of state. Oakley supposedly shot the ashes off a cigarette held by the newly crowned German Kaiser Wilhelm II at his request. Audiences were astounded to see her shooting a cigar from her husband's lips or splitting a playing-card edge-on at thirty paces, and she earned more than anyone except Buffalo Bill Cody himself.

No one depicted a witch in the way Margaret Hamilton did in the movie *The Wizard of Oz*. Hamilton played the role of the Wicked Witch of the West, opposite Judy Garland's character Dorothy Gale, creating not only her most famous role, but also one of the screen's most memorable villains. After the tornado swirled the Gale House into the air and it came back to earth, the house landed on the Wicked Witch of the East, killing her instantly. As people gather in astonishment, Glinda the Good Witch of the North reminds the Wicked Witch that the ruby slippers on the dead witch's feet have magic powers, and just as the Wicked Witch goes to grab them, the slippers disappear and miraculously reappear on Dorothy's feet. Who can forget when the Wicked Witch of the West said to Dorothy "I'll get you, my pretty, and your little dog, too!"

3

Halloween Trick-or-treat

These adorable children, surrounded by stocks and ears of Indian corn, are peering into the center of a jack o'lantern that has wide eyes and a huge gaping mouth. Pumpkins carved with ghoulish faces and illuminated by candles are a sure sign of the Halloween season. The practice of decorating jack o'lanterns originated in Ireland, where large turnips and mangelwurzels (a large beet) were hollowed out to act as lanterns. In fact, the name jack o'lantern comes from an Irish folktale about a man named Stingy Jack. When Jack died, he found himself barred from heaven as well as hell. But the devil took some pity on Jack, giving him an ember of coal to light his turnip lantern as he wandered between both places for eternity.

On this night of spooks and gnomes
Of swooning leaves and cringing crones
Of legends told from ear to ear
Of shrieking cats that grin and sneer

A dog is said to be man's best friend, and in this case a young boy and his spaniel dog peer into a candle illuminated jack o'lantern they had just carved.

When wild, ugly faces we carved in its skin,
Glaring out through the dark with a candle within!
When we laughed round the corn heap, with hearts all in tune,
Our chair a broad pumpkin,—our lantern the moon,
Telling tales of the fairy who traveled like steam
In a pumpkin-shell coach, with two rats for her team!

John Greenleaf Whittier

These boys' faces are illuminated from the candle lit jack o'lantern, that has diamond shaped eyes and nose and a multi-spiked smile. The holiday we know and love as Halloween had its roots in the Celtic festival of Samhain, during which people would light bonfires and dress up in costumes as a way to ward off spirits before All Saints' Day on November 1.

At twelve o'clock you must be ready,
And hold your pumpkin good and steady
For by its rays of candle light
One Halloween all things are bright!

These two youngsters have great expressions as they coo from behind four jack o'lanterns with ears of Indian corn in the foreground. Known as flint corn, and sometimes as calico corn, Indian corn is a variant of maize, the same species as common corn. However, because each kernel has a hard outer layer to protect the soft endosperm, it is likened to being as hard as flint, hence the name. Indian Corn has come to symbolize the harvest season; they crop up every fall with ears of corn with multicolored kernels that adorn front doors and grace holiday centerpieces.

Wish you were here with pumpkins of your own
For it's mo fun to see the ghosts and witches all alone

Why shouldn't the dog enjoy Halloween as well? Wearing a cat adorned witch's hat and holding a pumpkin candy holder, he's ready to follow the neighborhood children, who are off trick-or-treating, and hopefully get a dog biscuit for his treat.

On one mystic, magic night,
Jack O Lanterns glowing bright,
kids with bags of candy sweet,
roam door to door and street to street,
all dressed up for trick-or-treat!

This smiling young girl, sitting on a wood carved chest with a black cat and a jack o'lantern candy bucket, holds a Mickey Mouse mask in addition to a pumpkin turban and black face mask to protect her identity. The Mickey Mouse character had been created by Walt Disney and his designer-cartoonist Ub Iwerks, and has since become one of the most recognizable characters in the world. In 1978, in honor of his fiftieth anniversary, Mickey Mouse was to become the first cartoon character to have a star on the Hollywood Walk of Fame.

This young trick-or-treater is dressed in a witch's hat and a swastika printed costume, as she carries a jack o'lantern candy bucket and rides a corn broom. In Hinduism, the right-facing symbol (卐) is called a swastika, symbolizing *surya* (sun), prosperity, and good luck. However, before it was corrupted by the Nazi power in Germany, there was in the early twentieth century a huge fad for the swastika as a benign good luck symbol. The swastika remained a popular embroidery motif in Eastern Europe and Russia until its symbol of luck was forevermore corrupted.

This quartet of Halloween revelers are standing in front of the Scannell House at 489 Walnut Avenue in Jamaica Plain, ready to go trick-or-treating in 1925. From the left to right are Harry Skill and Robbie Sullivan, dressed as Spaniards, David Scannell, Jr. as a Spanish Gentleman in a powdered wig, and Gordon Scannell, dressed as Captain Kidd. The costumes look awfully professional, and Captain Kidd's posture is befitting that of a pirate! (Courtesy of Henry Scannell)

Florence Wilson visited Washington Street Police Station in Roslindale in 1940 for their annual Halloween celebration, and she won a camera that is handed to her by Captain Francis M. Tilman of Station 17, with a clown leaning over to admire it. Captain Tilman was the commander in charge District 17 and was stationed at West Roxbury. What better way for children to respect and appreciate the local policemen than to go to a party, with candy, that they hosted every Halloween.

A group of young children, some brandishing battery illuminated pumpkin lanterns on sticks, arrive at the steps of a house seeking Halloween treats. One has a pumpkin bucket for his candy while others have large brown bags, which obviously were meant to hold larger amounts of treats.

What better way to go trick-or-treating than with your parents dressed as robots. Though the child is dressed in a quilted jacket and khakis and looks at his robotic parent in awe, the parents got into the Halloween groove—in silver polyester jumpsuits, gloves, a two-handled mask, and a strap-on box on their chests—more than their son did. According to NASA, a robonaut is a dexterous humanoid robot built and designed at NASA Johnson Space Center in Houston, Texas. Working side by side with humans or going where the risks are too great for people, robonauts will expand our ability for construction and discovery.

The boy on the left is dressed as a record player cabinet with the Capitol Records of Canada record *All My Loving* by the Beatles on the front, ready to be played. The band, comprised of John Lennon, Paul McCartney, George Harrison, and Ringo Starr, is regarded to be among the most influential bands of all time. The record was released in 1963. It was immensely popular and made the Beatles into one of the foremost rock groups of the 1960s. In his 1980 *Playboy* interview, John Lennon said, "[I]t's a damn good piece of work ... But I play a pretty mean guitar in back."

Close your eyes and I'll kiss you
Tomorrow I'll miss you
Remember I'll always be true
And then while I'm away, I'll write home everyday
And I'll send all my loving to you

A group of children dressed in E.T. costumes descended upon Halloween in 1982. E.T. stands for the *E.T. - The Extra Terrestrial*, which was a science fiction movie produced and directed by Steven Spielberg and written by Melissa Mathison. It tells the story of Elliott, a boy who befriends an extraterrestrial, dubbed E.T., who is stranded on Earth. Along with his friends and family, Elliott must find a way to help E.T. return home while avoiding the government. Notice the homemade communicator used by E.T. to phone home, made from various parts including an umbrella lined with tinfoil, and a Martinson coffee can filled with other electronics.

An adorable young girl and her equally adorable pet dachshund dressed as a clown, knocks on a door as they seek a candy treat. Her shopping bag states "Treats or I Bite." It is always good to take along the family dog on Halloween night, and give him a dog treat as well!

Halloween is for dog population too.
They celebrate just like you.
The dogs that go bark in the night
The ones that cuddle humans tight

These three children, accompanied by their mother, visit a house trick-or-treating on Halloween, and the woman offers treats to the children from a silver candy dish. Though Halloween is thought to derive from the ancient Celtic festival of Samhain, the custom of trick-or-treating on Halloween might actually come from the belief that supernatural beings, or the souls of the dead, roamed the earth at this time and needed to be appeased. Thus, offering treats appeases not just the souls of the departed but also the sweet tooth of the children!

The look of joy on these children's faces is obvious as they stand in the doorway on Halloween. The boy has a poncho with a clown face embroidered on the front and a star embossed hat and the girl is dressed as a princess with a gilt paper crown. Look at the smile on that boy and the size of that candy bag with a skull smiling as widely as they are!

Trick-or-treat! Trick-or-treat!
Give me something good to eat.
Give me candy. Give me cake.
Give me something good to take.

These Halloween revelers are collecting donations for "Trick-or-treat for UNICEF" in 1967. The children are dressed in Halloween costumes, with UNICEF (United Nations International Children's Emergency Fund) arm bands and collection cartons. The coins collected in these cartons help to fund programs for needy children and mothers in countries worldwide. Mrs. Henry Johnson, on the left, hands her son Eric Johnson a UNICEF collection carton, as Mrs. Harold S. Horan, wife of 1967 UNICEF chairman, and Mrs. Sandy Wong adjust UNICEF identification arm bands on their children, Jenny Horan and Benjamin Wong.

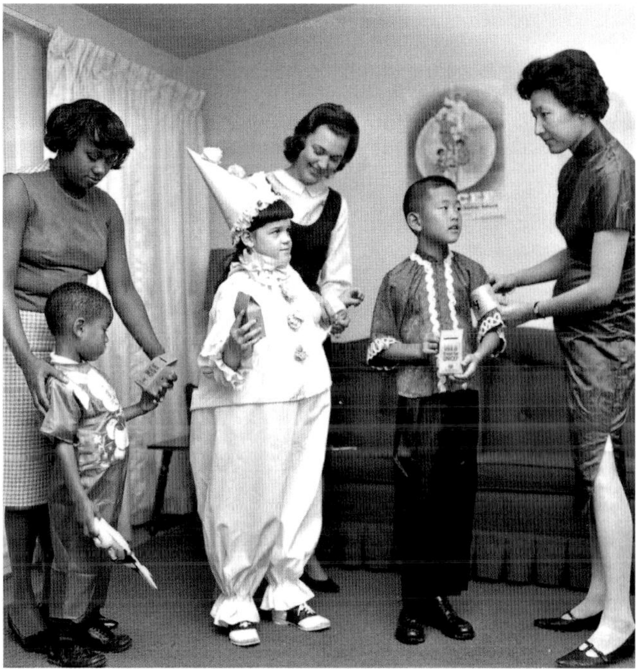

Holy Batmania! This group of Batboys and Batgirls are dressed and ready to protect Gotham in relation to the 1989 *Batman* movie, which starred Michael Keaton, and played in theaters continuously for almost six months! Batman was a beloved comic book character and he and his sidekick Robin were well known television characters in the immensely popular show. The catch phrases were "Batman has no limits" and Robin's "Holy ... " exclamations.

Garth, Glenn and Jerry Jernigan Jr. dressed identically as Tony the Tiger for Halloween and are seen posing for a photograph before they set out on visiting their neighborhood. Tony the Tiger was the advertising mascot for Kellogg's Frosted Flakes, a popular cereal, whose catchphrase saying, "They're g-r-r-reat!" was heard near and far. Since Tony's debut in 1952 by Eugene Kolkey, an accomplished graphics artist, the character that has spanned several generations and become a breakfast cereal icon. However, Esso (now Exxon Mobil) began using a similar tiger as a promotional mascot for gasoline products. Exxon then followed through with protocol and federally registered its tiger under the petroleum products category. Unlike the Kellogg slogan "They're gr-r-reat!" Esso also had a slogan, "Put a tiger in your tank."

Colonel Harland Sanders started a nationwide fast food restaurant known as Kentucky Fried Chicken. Though an attorney, his great claim to fame was his secret recipe of frying chicken that he first served in South Salt Lake, Utah. Within a few years the company was franchised with more than 600 locations across the United States. In 1964, Sanders sold the Kentucky Fried Chicken, but even after its sale it was still referred to as "the Colonel's chicken." These two trick or theaters dressed as Colonel Sanders, with a Colonel Sanders mask, white jackets, and black ties, and hold striped chicken buckets with a line portrait of the founder as their candy baskets.

This baby is dressed as Ruth Bader Ginsburg for Halloween. Wearing the trademark eyeglasses and lace jabot collar and holding a wood gavel, the child has a Baby Ruth candy bar in front of her on the highchair table. Ruth Bader Ginsburg was an attorney and jurist who served as an associate justice of the Supreme Court of the United States from 1993 until her death in September 2020. After a lifetime of flourishing in the face of adversity, she became an icon for empowered women who perceived her success as well deserved and something all should try to emulate. Supreme Court Justice Ginsburg proved time and again that she was a force to be reckoned with.

Raggedy Anne, Raggedy Andy, and Little Red Riding Hood are ready to go trick-or-treating. Raggedy Ann is a character created by Johnny Gruelle that appeared in a series of books he wrote and illustrated for young children. Raggedy Ann is a rag doll with red yarn for hair and a triangle nose as is her brother Andy. In 1941, the two characters were immortalized in the film *Raggedy Ann and Raggedy Andy.* Little Red Riding Hood is a fairytale character who walks through the woods to deliver food to her sickly grandmother but encounters the Big Bad Wolf who wants to eat the girl and the food in the basket. He sped to Grandmother's house and ate her, and when the girl arrives, she notices that her grandmother looks very strange. A woodsman who was chopping logs nearby heard her cries and ran towards the cottage as fast as he could. He grabbed the wolf and made him spit out the poor Grandmother, who was a bit frazzled by the whole experience, but still in one piece. The woodsman knocked out the wolf and carried him deep into the forest where he wouldn't bother people any longer.

Aliyha Alleyne, left, and Kadeem Dixon wear Lion King Simba Halloween costumes at the Franklin Park Zoo Howl in 1998. *The Lion King* is a movie by Walt Disney that premiered in 1994 and soon was adapted as a critically acclaimed Broadway musical, and later as a book, all showing how the lion takes his place in the circle of life. The popularity of this character was immense, and the beloved Simba became a popular icon; in fact, *The Lion King* revolves around Simba's relationship with his father, which is really "the real heart and emotional underpinning of the whole story." Simba is a Swahili word for lion, reflecting Simba's origins in Africa.

4

HALLOWEEN COSTUMES

Weldon's Fancy Dress for Children had 200 designs, many in color, that could be worn to Carnival Galas and Pageants. The cover of the booklet had four children dressed, from left to right, as a Pearly King, a shepherdess, a Japanese woman in a kimono, and a pirate. Walter Weldon, a former journalist in London, founded *Weldon's Fashion Journal* and his publications in the late nineteenth century were through Weldon & Company, a pattern company which produced hundreds of patterns and projects for numerous types of Victorian needlework. *Weldon's Ladies' Journal,* published from 1875 to1954, supplied dressmaking patterns for both day and evening wear. By the 1920s, Weldon's offered a variety of patterns that could be sewn by hand or on a sewing machine at home.

The Gibson Art Company offered *Halloween Decorations and Party Goods*, with a smiling orange and black cat on the booklet cover. Founded in 1850 by the Gibson Brothers in Cincinnati, Ohio, they originally operated a lithographic and copperplate engraving business that produced printed bonds, stock certificates, checks, business cards, and labels. The company was later purchased by Robert Gibson, and he is credited with popularizing the "French Fold" card, one sheet of paper folded in half twice, which became the best-selling greeting card form and thereafter an industry standard. Gibson did not just produce greeting cards, but also Halloween decorations. Today, Gibson Greetings, Inc. designs and sells greeting cards, paper party wares, gift wrap, and related specialty relationship-fostering products which are sold in retail outlets worldwide.

Costumes for Halloween were often some of the most interesting Halloween creations for men and women, especially if they were in black and orange as the predominant colors. With fanciful hats, some with dangling jack o'lanterns, a sheer moon and star bedecked chiffon overlay, smocks with grimacing moon faces and a skirt decorated with jack o'lanterns, each design was sure to be noticed at the Halloween Dance.

Nina R. Jordan offered directions on how to make a Black Cat Mask for Halloween, along with crepe paper caps, a pumpkin seed necklace, a balloon in a paper hat and a cardboard witch on a broom. Jordan was a multi-talented artist and handicrafter and illustrated her book *Holiday Handicraft* as well as *The Gingerbread Boy* by Eunice Tietjens. In the magazine *Child Life*, she shows children how to make Halloween decorations. As she said, “When nimble brains and busy fingers begin their preparations for Halloween pranks, something surprising is bound to happen, and everyone is sure to have a beautiful time.”

In 1928, the Kirchhof Patent Company offered a new Halloween line of brightly colored Halloween Crickets, Twirly Clicks, and Halloween Jumbo Rattlers that could be heard from near and far as you and your friends twirled them. The company was founded in 1865 in Newark, New Jersey, and remained in the Kirchhof Reinhardt Dietze family until 1965 when it was sold to the Green Duck Company. The Kirchhof Company was an early manufacturer of Christmas tree candle holders, return-wheels, which was to later become more popularly known as the yo-yo, and these brightly colored noisemakers. The company also manufactured crickets that were used by the Allied soldiers at the landing of Normandy Beach during World War II.

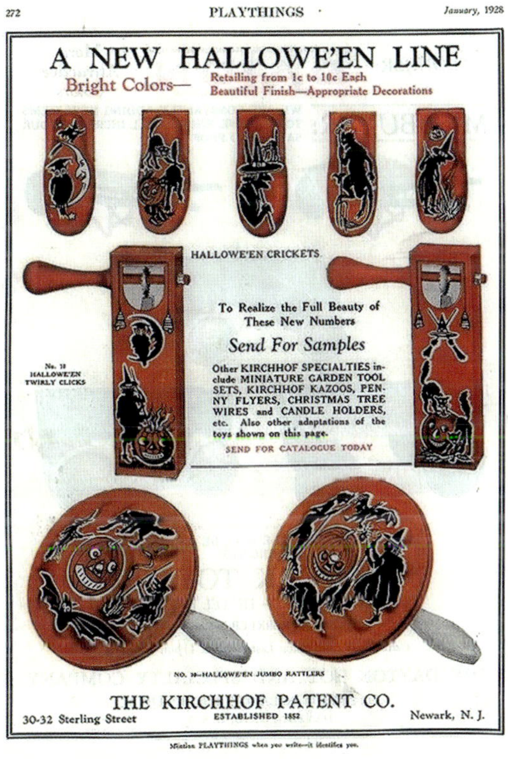

Two young women admire the Halloween decorations and novelties displayed in this store window that offered paper pumpkins, dancing skeletons, masks, party hats, and even a paper Turkey for Thanksgiving, ready to decorate the home for the holidays.

Two women set up a display of Halloween novelties including jack o'lanterns, masks, and costumes. The jack o'lanterns in the foreground were made of wax, with a candle inside to illuminate their faces in window display or on the front stairs. The larger plastic pumpkins were buckets for trick-or-treaters to carry the candy they received as they went from house to house trick-or-treating.

Playing with a jointed cardboard skeleton which was introduced by Beistle, a company founded in 1900 in Pennsylvania by Martin Luther Beistle. These girls are surrounded by all sorts of decorations that could be used to decorate not only one's home but a dance hall for a Halloween-themed dance. Orange paper balls that looked like pumpkins, paper skeletons, witches, owls, black cats, and many other decorations could be a fun way to decorate for a Halloween party.

This store is ready for both adults and children seeking the perfect Halloween costume. As the sign says, "Whoooooooo will you be on Halloween?" With costumes on a circular rack on the left and masks and novelty items in the display case, it also offered a basket of candy on the counter.

As the sign says, "Everything for Hallowe'en!" With plastic masks priced from 10 cents to 29 cents, it was fun to choose one to wear on Halloween night. Costumes for both Tiny Tots and children were $1.98 and they ran the gamut from skeletons, princesses, pirates, clowns, and a variety of other characters.

Jack's Joke Shop in Boston had a whole wall covered with latex Halloween masks of the famous and not-so-famous, including politicians, animals, monsters, or even Cleopatra or Marilyn Monroe. Founded in 1922 and originally located in Scollay Square, the store later moved to Tremont Street, where it was a destination for those seeking a wide variety of tricks, jokes, novelties, and magic supplies, as well as theatrical supplies including costumes, makeup, and wigs.

F. W. Woolworth's offered Halloween thrills and trick-or-treat fun, with fabric costumes that everybody and every budget could afford with costumes such as a skeleton, Donald Duck, or a witch. They said their "Halloween masks look almost real" and were delightful to fearsome, in vivid colors in a huge assortment of gauze and lightweight rubber masks. While there, why not pick up "Two-for-the-Money Treats" which were Halloween toys with delicious pops that included a horn, a pumpkin, a witch, a clarinet, and motorcycle.

The 1966 Collegeville Costumes A-200 Assortment offered Halloween costumes that had shed resistant sparkle embossed velvet decorations, "pretty girl" costumes of flame-retardant rayon and vinyl character masks with wide-vision eye holes. Seen here are the Honey Bunny, Doctor Solar, Astronaut, Rag Doll, Captain U.S.A., Blue Fairy, Tiger, Witch, and the Starlight Princess costumes.

Sears offered Halloween costumes that went the gamut from a nurse, ballerina, majorette, princess, and Miss America contestant (complete with tiara) to a race driver, chief, Marine, and trooper. However, their famous fantasy characters allowed a child to dress so "your friends won't recognize you behind the vinyl masks!" Seen here is a Batman, Superman, and Mickey Mouse Halloween costume.

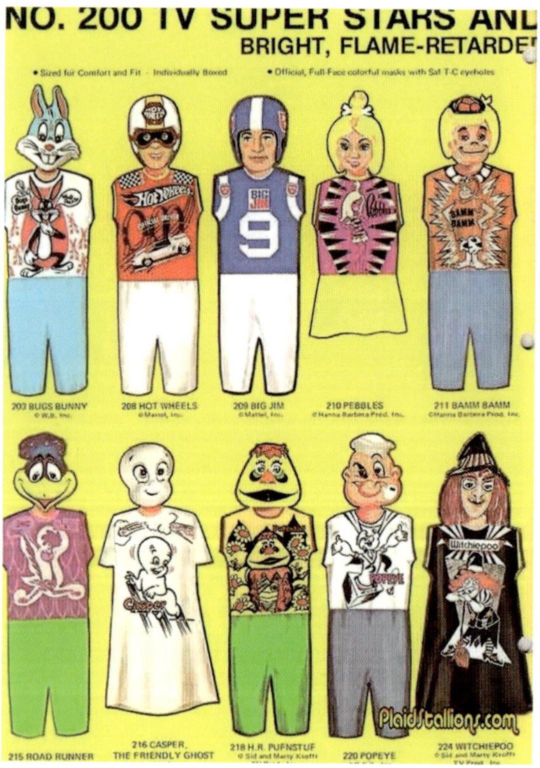

Collegeville Costumes offered bright, flame retardant costumes that were sized for comfort and fit with full face masks with Sat T-C eye holes. A child could choose to be Bugs Bunny, Hot Wheels, Big Jim, Pebbles, Bamm Bamm, Road Runner, Casper the Friendly Ghost, H. R. Pufnstuf, Popeye, or even Witchiepoo.

One can almost hear the melodic song "*Chim chiminey, Chim chiminey, Chim chim cher-ee! A sweep is as lucky as lucky can be*" by songwriters Richard M. Sherman and Robert B. Sherman with these two Halloween revelers dressed as Bert Dawes and Mary Poppins from the popular movie *Mary Poppins*. The British folklore attributed to chimney sweeps is that shaking hands with one could bring a person good luck, as well as an ash covered hand. So, with a chimney sweep broom, a liberal dusting of coal dust, and a trusty umbrella and magic carpet bag, you too could become the characters from the 1964 Disney movie which has since become a classic.

Have Gun-Will Travel was the motto of Paladin. Beginning in 1958, this was a popular Western television series starring Richard Boone and Kam Tong that was produced and originally broadcast on both television as well as radio. The television version of the series was rated number three in the Nielsen ratings every year of its first four seasons, and it is one of the few shows in television history to spawn a successful radio version. So, with this five-piece outfit, including a vest, mask, tie, tiering, and belt slide, what young boy wouldn't be proud to be Paladin on Halloween?

This is a Halloween mask of Krampus, and there seems to be little doubt as to the true identity of Krampus, as in no other form is the full regalia of the Horned God of the Witches so well preserved. His jagged teeth and lolling tongue, furled wrinkled forehead and horns, and the birch switches he used may have a connection with the initiation rites of certain witch covens, rites which entailed binding and scourging as a form of mock-death. The chains on his limbs are thought to symbolize the binding of the Devil by the Christian Church. With this mask, yell "Üdvöslet *a Krampusztól!*" which is Hungarian for "Greetings from the Krampus."

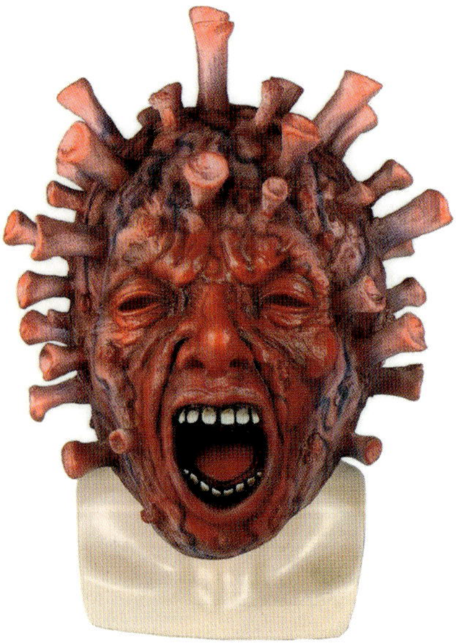

This vinyl mask represents the coronavirus. It had been strongly suggested that all people wear a face covering to not only protect oneself but the community, as you could have COVID-19 and not know it. In 2020 and 2021, everyone needed to wear a face covering, even ghosts and goblins! However, this somewhat distasteful face mask with a screaming head with protruding growths covering the head and ears was offered on eBay for a Halloween reveler who wanted to make a statement. It was scary not just as a Halloween mask but as a representation of the pandemic that swept the world.

5

Halloween Candy and Treats

A smiling Mary Ann Sammartino Nagle of Phillips Chocolates displays some of the Halloween themed candy including milk, white, and dark chocolate skull lollipops! Phillips Chocolates was founded in 1925 by Phillip and Concettina DiMare Strazzula, and they began selling chocolate out of their home in the fall of 1925, eventually opening a shop in Belmont in 1935 known as Phillips Sweets. Now located on Morrissey Boulevard in Dorchester, Massachusetts, the Colonial-inspired candy shop was opened in 1952 by brothers Matthew and Philip Strazzula and brother-in-law Joseph Sammartino. Phillips Chocolates is Boston's oldest chocolatier and is run by the third and fourth generation cousins Joseph Sammartino, Jr., and Philip Strazzula III, and Joe's son, Matthew Sammartino. (Courtesy of Phillips Chocolates)

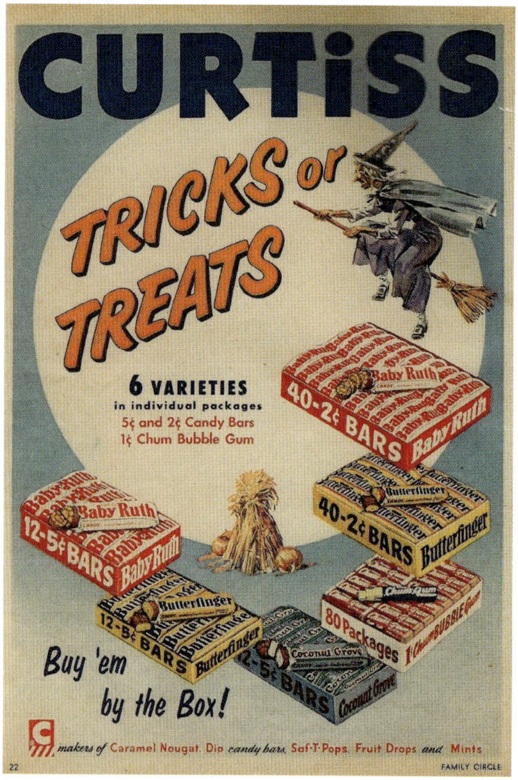

Curtiss Candy offered treats in six varieties, with Baby Ruth, Butterfinger, 5-cent bars, Coconut Grove, Chum Bubble gum, and 2-cent bars. Founded in 1916 by Otto Schnering, he named the new candy company using his mother's maiden name because of anti-German feelings during World War I. The first candy made was Kandy Kake, later renamed in 1920 as the log-shaped Baby Ruth candy bar. The second candy made was the chocolate-covered peanut butter crunch Butterfinger, which was introduced in 1926. Over the years, Curtiss was the maker of Caramel Nougat and Dip candy bars, Saf-T-Pops, Fruit Drops, and Mints. In 1964, Standard Brands purchased Curtiss Candy Company. Standard Brands merged with Nabisco in 1981 and in 1990, Nabisco sold the Curtiss brands to Nestlé.

There would be no tricks if you treat 'em right with Curtiss Halloween Candies. A trio of trick-or-treaters dressed as a clown, a lady in a mink stole, and a ghost fly on a corn whisk broom with their trick-or-treat bags filled to the brim with Curtiss Candy. As they said, "When little goblins sweep down on Halloween, be ready with their favorite Curtiss Candies such as Baby Ruth Bars, Chum Gum, Saf-T-Pops, Caramel Rolls, and Butterfingers. Better load up now, because there will be "no tricks if you treat 'em right!"

Brach's Candy was founded by Emil J. Brach in Chicago in 1904 and he named it Brach's Palace of Sweets. Brach's produced several candy bars, including a chocolate-covered, honeycombed, peanut butter Swing Bar, Bullies, Jots, as well as a mint and almond nougat bar. In the late 1940s, the company concentrated on bulk and bagged candies, as Halloween trick-or-treating became a popular activity. Brach's promoted its candy corn and other fall-themed candies. Seen here a group of trick-or-treaters stand on the walkway and say, "This is the house that has Brach's ... Somebody ring the doorbell!"

Treat 'em to delicious Just-for-Halloween Candies, fresh from Brach's. As the advertisement says "Little masqueraders love to be greeted with a heaping variety of Brach's Halloween Candies. So many different kinds to pick and choose! Everything from luscious bars and lollipops to cute miniature pumpkins. *Special* candies, right in the spirit of Halloween. Shop for Brach's at your store this week, and *do* get an assortment. You'll delight the kids!" The boy, in a pirate outfit with eye patch, red polka dot bandanna, and a ship anchor tattoo, reaches for a piece of candy from a bountiful display.

A woman offers Baby Ruth and Butterfinger candy bars to two trick-or-treaters. Dressed as a witch and a bunny rabbit, these two children smile at the candy as their bags say, "Tricks or Treats." A Baby Ruth is a candy bar made of peanuts, caramel, and milk chocolate-flavored nougat, covered in compound chocolate, and a Butterfinger is a candy bar made by Nestle. The bar consists of a flaky, crisp orange-colored, peanut butter-flavored center that is coated in compound chocolate. Either choice was a good one!

What a sweet surprise! Baby Ruth candy is not only delicious, but it helps replenish energy and peps you up. Although the name of the candy bar sounds like the name of the famous baseball player Babe Ruth, the Curtiss Candy Company said that it was named after President Grover Cleveland's daughter Ruth Cleveland. The candy maker, located on the same street as Wrigley Field, named the bar "Baby Ruth" in 1921, ironically as Babe Ruth's fame grew, and many years after Cleveland had left the White House, and interestingly after his daughter had died. However, the company did not negotiate an endorsement deal with Ruth, and many saw the company's story about the origin of the name to be a devious way to avoid having to pay the baseball player any royalties.

Schrafft's Chocolate Company was founded by in 1861 by William F. Schrafft, who began by making gumdrops and candy canes. A landmark in Sullivan Square in Charlestown, Massachusetts, Schrafft's in their heyday was the largest general line confectioner in the country and employed over 1,600 workers including my great uncle, Dominic Giannelli, a master candy maker. The famous Schrafft's building, built in 1928, has a large neon sign that is still a landmark in the city of Boston. Here Schrafft's offered Peppermint Patty, chocolate covered Caramallow Bar, and chocolate covered marshmallow as a treat instead of a trick.

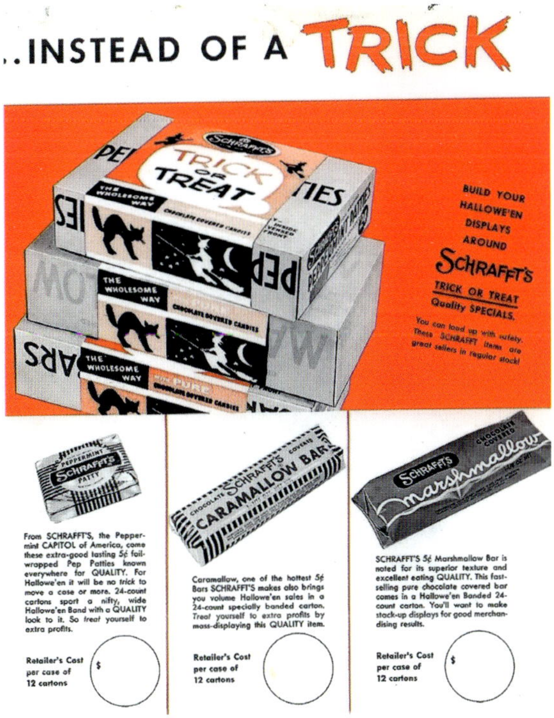

Here Kiddie, Kiddie, Kiddie! The Milky Way candy bar was a delicious candy made from milk chocolate, golden caramel, and creamy chocolate malted milk nougat. Milky Way was created by Frank C. Mars and was manufactured since 1923 in Minneapolis, Minnesota, the name and taste derived from a then popular malted milkshake of the day. In 1935, Mars adopted the marketing slogan, "The sweet you can eat between meals," later using "At work, rest and play, you get three great tastes in a Milky Way." Immensely popular, the candy bar is still manufactured and marketed by the Mars Confectionary company.

Sweet Stalkin'! Mars was said to be the family choice for candy. Here, a trick-or-treater dressed as a clown watches as a haystack eats a Mar's Milky Way candy bar. When "Tricks or treats?" is the question, here are two perfect answers: Get Mars 6-packs and Mars "24s." However, whichever size you chose, there were two variants available: chocolate nougat with milk chocolate coating, and vanilla nougat with a dark chocolate coating, each originally selling for five cents. In June 1932, the bar was marketed as a two-piece bar, and four years later, in 1936, the chocolate and vanilla were separated. The vanilla version, with a dark chocolate coating, was called "Forever Yours," and marketed until 1979.

Be good to your goblins! Carlton's Halloween Treats were marshmallow wrapped treats. This late 1950s Halloween Marshmallow Witch Candy box shows a smiling witch riding her broomstick over a neighborhood on Halloween night. Marshmallows are made of gelatin and sugar, with a dusty powdered sugar surface, and they squish like a sponge when you squeeze or bite down on them. This package of marshmallow witches has eighty individually wrapped treats at a penny apiece, hopefully enough for the trick-or-treaters!

Nestlé Milk Chocolate bar was the perfect treat on Halloween. The candy was invented by Henri Nestlé in 1875 in Vevey, Switzerland, and was created as a competitor to the well-known Hershey milk chocolate bar. Heinrich Nestle was a Frenchman who was officially authorized in Lausanne, Vaud, to perform chemical experiments, make up prescriptions, and sell medicines. During this time, he changed his name to Henri Nestlé in order to adapt better to the new social environment in Vevey, where he eventually settled. Nestlé's milk-condensation process enabled the chocolatier Daniel Peter to perfect his milk chocolate formulation in 1875, after seven years of effort, and the two men subsequently formed a partnership which resulted, four years later, in 1879, in the organization of the Nestlé Company, which eventually became one of the largest Europe-based confection industries. Nestlé Milk Chocolate candy bars are solid chocolate goodness.

PEZ was first marketed as a compressed peppermint sweet in Vienna, Austria, in 1927 by Eduard Haas. The name PEZ is an abbreviation of Pfefferminz, the German word for peppermint. The first PEZ dispensers were similar in size and shape to a cigarette lighter and dispensed an adult breath mint marketed as an alternative to tobacco; they were invented by Oscar Uxa. Haas Food Manufacturing Corporation of Vienna was the first to sell PEZ products and toy character head dispensers were introduced in 1955, after the candy was introduced in the United States. There are over 550 unique dispenser heads with thousands of variations. In the mid-1970s, three historical figures were created: Bestsy Ross, Paul Revere, and Daniel Boone, which were released as part of the Bicentennial of the United States series. Here a witch face surmounts a PEZ dispenser saying "Kids! Halloween Time is PEZ Time."

Everybody's favorite goblin wanted a treat, but "this new Necco treat does the trick, too!" The New England Confectionery Company was founded in 1847 by Oliver Chase, who invented a lozenge cutting machine with which he produced thin wafers. At the time of the Civil War, these were called "hub wafers" and were enjoyed by Civil War soldiers. In 1901, Chase and Company merged with Ball and Fobes and Bird, Wright, and Company to incorporate the New England Confectionery Company. Commonly referred to as Necco and by 1912, the wafers were being advertised as "Necco Wafers" in eight delicious flavors.

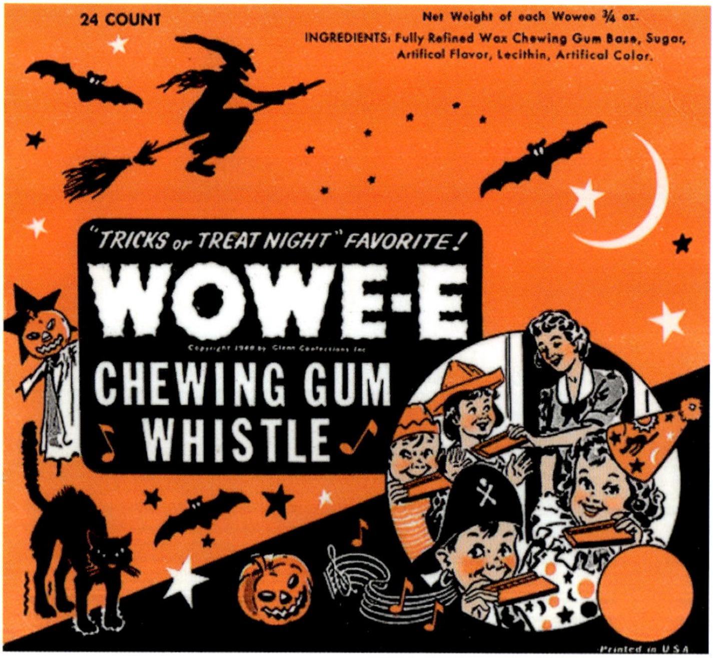

The WOWE-E Chewing Gum whistle allowed trick-or-treaters to make glorious music on the wax whistle before they popped it in their mouth as chewing gum. The unique harmonica-themed candy was produced by John W. Glenn of Glenn Confectioners in Buffalo, New York, beginning in 1923. The candy was made with orange wax that could be chewed like gum. As one aficionado said, "That Wowe-e whistle was the best thing since sliced bread. It had that sweet taste to it and once you started chewing on it, you almost couldn't help yourself but to swallow some of it."

Wrigley's Spearmint gum, in a bewitching mint leaf flavor, advertised "the flavor lasts." Wrigley's Spearmint is a brand of Wrigley's chewing gum. William Wrigley, Jr. launched the brand in 1893 and markets the gum as its classic brand, although the company's brand Juicy Fruit has been on the market slightly longer. In 1911, Wrigley took over Zeno Manufacturing, the company that made his chewing gum, and established the Wm. Wrigley Jr. Company.

Cracker Jack, with Cracker Jack's mascots Sailor Jack and his dog Bingo on the package, was advertised as "The trick that makes the perfect treat—anytime!" Cracker Jack was started by the Rueckheim Brothers who produced a recipe that included popcorn, peanuts, and molasses, and was first presented to the public at the World's Colombian Exposition in Chicago in 1893. It was packaged with a prize of trivial value inside. The Cracker Jack name and slogan—"The More You Eat The More You Want"—were registered in 1896 and it was named by an enthusiastic sampler who remarked: "That's a crackerjack!" Crackerjack is a colloquialism meaning "of excellent quality."

Luden's Confectionery was started by William H. Luden in 1879, and he produced cough drops as well as candy. In 1928, the company was acquired by Food Industries of Philadelphia, and Luden's would produce more than 500 varieties of candy in addition to its better-known cough drops. Seen here in 1970, this trio—a ghost, a witch with her broom, and hobo—said, "After carefully surveying the market, we recommend stocking 5th Avenue and Nut Log as the way to wrap up Halloween."

This trick-or-treater seems delighted to choose a Post Alpha-Bits oat cereal box from the Post Treat-Pak on Halloween. Post was founded by Charles W. Post in Battle Creek, Michigan, in 1895. He was inspired to start his food company marketing breakfast cereals. Post's first product was Postum, a cereal beverage alternative to coffee made from wheat and molasses. Grape Nuts, the first cereal, was developed in 1897. The company grew tremendously and after acquiring Jell-O gelatin in 1925, Baker's Chocolate in 1927, Maxwell House coffee in 1928, and other food brands, changed its name to General Foods Corporation. This young boy, however, could choose from Sugar Crisp, Sugar Rice Krinkles, or Alpha-Bits. As the ad says, "All Post cereals happen to be just a little bit better."

6

Halloween Parties and Games

The *Halloween Fate Game*, with black bats, stars, and crescent moons decorating the four corners, was a game of fate of fortune made by the Beistle Company, and by spinning the dial it told you one of sixteen fates that would befall you on Halloween. With such fates as "Your dog will eat your homework," "A bat will steal your hat," "Eat an apple every day, or your teeth will fall out," and "If you wake up late tomorrow, eat a lemon," they were peculiar fates to predict. So, spin the wheel and find out your fate!

This witch, wearing her witch's hat and with her cauldron and stick, is stirring her "Witches Brew!" The brew might be a potent magical concoction of herbs, or a harmful concoction including an eye of newt. However, she looks like a harmless witch, and maybe her brew is actually a refreshing mixture of ginger ale, pineapple juice, and lemon juice along with scoops of lime sherbet cooled with dry ice that created a beguiling smoke effect. The men in the background, in their white serving jackets and fanciful masks, are awaiting the moment the brew is ready to be served to guests.

The Witch's Brew written in Shakespeare's Macbeth was composed of "Fillet of a fenny snake, In the cauldron boil and bake; Eye of newt and toe of frog, Wool of bat and tongue of dog, Adder's fork and blind-worm's sting, Lizard's leg and owlet's wing, For a charm of powerful trouble, Like a hell-broth boil and bubble."

A young hostess greets her costumed and masked friends for a Halloween party, with a cautionary sign on the door that states "Beware, Ghosts are within." In the twentieth century children's parties would suggest to "have the hall totally dark with the door ajar with no one in sight to welcome the guests. As they step in, they are surprised to be greeted by someone dressed as a ghost who extends his hand which is covered with wet salt." Another instructed hosts to dress like a "shade," or a resident of the underworld, to welcome guests. Whatever one did, it was fun to tell spooky stories, sing songs, compete for prizes, and enjoy ghost sandwiches and goblin cookies.

A pie eating contest at a teen Halloween party was one sure way to have fun or make a mess of one's face and costume. Small pies in various flavors were covered in mounds of whipped cream, often with a cherry at the top. Once given the signal, the young party goers eat the pies as fast as they can, but they cannot use their hands, which are clasped behind their backs! The winner of the pie eating contest might have a cream and pie covered face as well as an upset stomach by midnight.

Did you know that fortunes could be told by using apple seeds? Well in 1952, this advertisement said that if one counted the seeds of the apple before eating it, you might identify your career or wealth. Each person was given an apple and after cutting it, removed the seeds and carefully counted them. If one seed was found you were a rich man, two seeds a poor man, three seeds a beggar man, four seeds a thief, five seeds a doctor, six seeds a lawyer, and seven seeds a merchant. So, count the seeds carefully!

One, I love; two, I love;
Three, I love, I say;
Four, I love with all my heart;
Five, I cast away;
Six, he loves;
Seven, she loves
Eight, they both agree;
Nine, he comes;
Ten, he tarries:
Eleven, he courts;
Twelve, he marries.

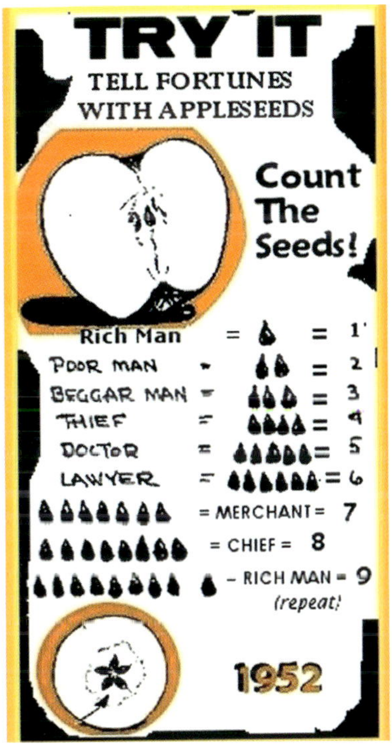

The Black Cat Fortune Telling Game was copyrighted by Parker Brothers in Salem in 1897 and had a black cat with a red bow tie on the box cover. The game includes four sets of six cards each related to a suit (hearts, diamonds, spades, and clubs) with images of cats on the obverse and fortunes printed on the reverse. The cards are used to foretell everything from the future, present, past, danger, general advice and love matters. The Black Cat Fortune Telling game is different from other types of fortune telling cards such as tarot cards. Several people can play as a group, with players reading each other's fortunes. There is no declared winner or loser, just a lot of fun for all who play.

This colorful Halloween *Pick a Pumpkin* fortune wheel had twelve jack o'lanterns with various faces and a scene of a witch with an elfin creature, obviously holding a book of spells, a bat, and an owl in the light of a full moon, which is without a doubt brilliant. The game was made of mid-weight cardboard in Germany in the 1920s. Each of the tear-off pumpkins bear a fortune printed on the rear.

Pick a pumpkin and on its back you'll find your future bright or black

Witzi Wits, the Fortune Teller and her box of stunts for parties had a smiling witch, with an owl perched on her outstretched arm and the other holding her broom as she stands behind a steaming cauldron. This box of stunts, with fortune telling and a game of forfeits, was a board game produced by Alderman Fairchild Company in 1928 and includes fortune telling, a game of forfeits, lucky cards, and party suggestions.

The fortune teller foretold
Of heartache and of cold
Like the fates of something old
She said she knew things untold

The circular dial of *Witzi Wits, the Fortune Teller* allowed those playing the game to spin for their fortune. Fortunes such as "Will my lover ever propose to me?"; "Do you think 'social climber' would apply to me?"; "Will I be successful in society?"; or "Will I be an old maid?" were poignant questions. But there was a Lucky Spot at Number 8 with a jack o'lantern and swastikas, a left-facing symbol (卍) which has long symbolized the tantric aspects and female power of the goddess Kali, who is referred to in Hindu as "She Who is Death." Obviously, when the arrow fell on Number 8, one got a free spin!

The *Hand of Fate Fortune Telling Game* is a board game that was manufactured by McLoughlin Brothers in 1901. The cover of the box has a young bespectacled girl dressed in a witch costume with a peaked red hat and a cape, reading to a black cat, both inside a ring with symbols of the zodiac. Around the ring are black cats, bats, and owls. The Hand of Fate was a popular parlor games that piqued Victorians' fascination with mysticism. The magnetic dial at the center could be employed to play different games depending on which of the surrounding rings is used. The innermost circle allows the "hand" to answer historical questions, the middle circle provides character readings based on a player's birthday, and the outer circle of numbers lets players ask true or false questions, with even numbers representing true and uneven numbers false.

Fortunes by the Luminous Spirit was produced by the American Novelty Company in the 1940s as "spirited fun for parties of young and old." The center of this game has a witch riding her broom, which acts as an arrow to point to one of the twelve fortunes. The odd charms, symbols, and creatures include a ghost, bat, devil, and snake. The game stated that it would "glow in the dark after 2 minutes exposure to bright light."

The spirit-world around this world of sense
Floats like an atmosphere, and everywhere
Wafts through these earthly mists and vapors dense
A vital breath of more ethereal air.

Longfellow

The *Jack o'lantern Fortune Game* was introduced by the Beistle Company in the 1930s and could be played by both boys and girls with each having separate fortunes listed below. The Beistle Company, founded by Martin Luther Beistle in Pennsylvania in 1900, became known for manufacturing a variety of holiday decorations and party goods and was particularly well known for its catalog of Halloween decorations. In the game, sixteen fortunes were printed on the base and on the front are two numbered wheel spinners attached with eyelets. When the dials are spun, the numbers revel through the jack o' lantern's eyes and the corresponding fortune is listed below for girls on the left and boys on the right.

No real hostess in the 1960s would be without a spider web skirt to entertain her family and friends on Halloween night. Maybe she was channeling Elwyn Brooks White's book *Charlotte's Webb*, in which Wilbur the pig is befriended by a spider named Charlotte, whose web was woven in a barn doorway overlooking Wilbur's enclosure. When Wilbur discovers that he is being raised for slaughter, she promises to hatch a plan guaranteed to spare his life. What better way to make a Halloween fashion statement than by wearing a spider web skirt?

Flutter, flutter little bat,
How I wonder where you're at.
Swooping through the darkest night -
You find your way without a light.
Flutter, flutter little bat,
How I wonder where you're at!

Leanne Guenther

What better beverage was there to serve at a Halloween party than Rheingold Extra Dry Lager Beer. Seen here decorating a pumpkin with red pepper eyes, green bean lips, straw hair, and a witch's hat is the smiling hostess Nancy Woodruff, in a Bergdorf Goodman silk day dress, who was Miss Rheingold in 1955. Started in 1883 by the Liebmann family in New York, the beer was said to be a clean, clear dry beer and was advertised as "It's a beer as beer should taste! Always refreshing, never filling."

Schlitz was advertised as "the Beer that made Milwaukee famous" and was founded by August Krug in 1849 in Wisconsin. Around 1860 Joseph Schlitz, a former employee, married Krug's widow and began Jos. Schlitz Brewing Company. A young couple carve a jack o'lantern as they enjoy "leisure's light refresher." Today, Pabst Brewing Company, the successor to Schlitz, continues to produce Schlitz beer, Old Milwaukee, and four Schlitz malt liquors—Schlitz Red Bull, Schlitz Bull Ice, Schlitz High Gravity, and Schlitz Malt Liquor. As advertised, Schlitz leaves you feeling refreshed without feeling full. Light refreshment is half the fun!

This foursome is enjoying a Halloween dinner, with party hats and party horns of pumpkin faces that make sounds when blown. The table decorations are orange, black, and brown, and in the center of the table is a jack o'lantern wearing a witch's hat with vivid blue eyes, flanked by orange candles. The dessert follows the Halloween themed dinner and is a half orange shell cut in a jagged edge and filled with orange sherbet and fruit.

What better food to serve at your Halloween Party than Armour Star "Weeny Witch" skinless frankfurters? As the advertisement says, "Your goblins will gobble 'em ... " Founded by the Armour Brothers, headed by Philip Danforth Armour in 1863 in Chicago, it was to become Chicago's most important business and had helped make Chicago and its Union Stock Yards the center of America's meatpacking industry. Among the wide variety of meats marketed by Armour Star were these frankfurters that were said to have an "open fire" flavor.

Dessert at a Spooky Halloween Party might include this bewitching Midnight Cake. As the advertisement said: "Have a Spooky Hallowe'en Party ... and serve this cake!" The Devil's Food cake was strikingly as dark as midnight and deliciously moist, tender, and light with a snowy white icing. The advertisement shows the luscious cake with witches on brooms hovering over it as the Harvest moon rises in the background.

Midnight Cake

2 1/4 cups all-purpose flour
3/4 cup cocoa
1 1/4 teaspoons baking soda
3/4 teaspoon salt
1/4 teaspoon baking powder
1 1/2 cups sugar
3/4 cup butter, softened
2 eggs
3/4 cup water
3/4 cup black coffee
1 teaspoon vanilla extract

Whisk together the flour, cocoa, baking soda, salt and baking in a bowl. Set aside. Cream the sugar, butter and eggs in a large bowl using mixer. Add flour mixture to creamed mixture along with water, coffee and vanilla extract. Mix with mixer. Spray a 9 by 13 inch baking pan with cooking spray, add cake batter and bake in preheated 350 degree oven for 40 to 45 minutes until center tests done. Frost with buttercream frosting.

Bewitching Hallowe'en Surprises! Desserts can be extra rich and luscious if made with Baker's Chocolate and Cocoa. Founded in 1780 by Dr. James Baker in Dorchester Lower Mills, Baker's Chocolate is the oldest manufacturer of chocolate in the United States. In this advertisement, Halloween treats include Enchanted Chocolate Cake and Jack O'Lantern Yum Yums. As it was said: "Only Baker's Chocolate can give them such moist tenderness ... such appetizing color ... such rich chocolate taste." On the lower left was a coupon to send for a free Baker's "Sampler" book of famous chocolate recipes that were sure to impress family and friends.

7

Halloween Greetings

Halloween Night, seen in 1913 in a surreal design by John Winsch, was a card depicting a star filled night with a young girl sitting on a pumpkin as a procession of strangely odd figures parade before her. John O. Winsch began his career as a lithography clerk at the turn of the twentieth century, and by 1907 he was promoted to co-manager of the Art Lithographic Publishing Company, a position he held until 1915. After the British blockade of Germany during World War I prevented imports of greeting cards and postcards to the United States, Winsch became manager of the International Art Company.

Strange things will happen!
Strange things be seen!
If you'll watch out
On Hallowe'en!

George Clarkson Whitney, a Worcester native and Civil War veteran, took over his brother Sumner Whitney's stationery store in the 1870s and renamed it the Whitney Valentine Company. He became so successful that he bought out other local competitors, including Esther Howland, and the business became immensely successful. Whitney's motto was "Industry, punctuality and Christianity" and it was he who would make Worcester, Massachusetts, known as the heart of the American valentine-making industry. By the early twentieth century, his company was producing a wide variety of holiday cards. The Halloween cards were traditional as well as fanciful.

Hallowe'en Greetings had a beautiful witch canoodling with a very happy jack o'lantern. The look on that pumpkin's face is undeniable as her beauty is as beguiling, as is her ribbon dressed witch's hat.

BOO!
B is for broomsticks witches to fly,
O is outrageous spooks that go by,
O is for orange pumpkins so bright,
These are the signs of a Halloween night!

Hallowe'en Greetings had a young girl dressed as a witch with a witch's hat and black cape, with her broom at the ready, sitting on a pumpkin with two black cats accompanying her.

May Hallowe'en frolics engage you to-night
And your future by witches predicted, be bright

A little boy holds a jack o'lantern on Halloween. Wish you were here with pumpkins of your own for it's no fun to see the ghosts and witches all alone.

Jack-o-lantern pumpkin head he is a fearful sight.
If I were you, I'd be afraid to meet him in the night.
By day he is a pumpkin, but just you wait 'til night.
When out of eyes and nose and mouth there shines a yellow light.

The famous artist Norman Rockwell once said, “Maybe as I grew up and found the world wasn’t the perfect place I had thought it to be, I unconsciously decided that if it wasn’t an ideal world, it should be, and so painted only the ideal aspects of it.” Rockwell’s paintings of various holidays, among them Halloween, have become icons of American life in the twentieth century.

Norman Rockwell depicted this well-dressed couple in 1920 using an Ouija board to guess their future fate together. Will the spirits tell them of their future in a positive or negative response? William Fuld produced boards under the name “Ouija, claiming he learned the name ‘Ouija’ from using the board and that it was an ancient Egyptian word meaning ‘good luck.’” Fuld popularized the more widely accepted etymology: that the name came from a combination of the French and German words for “yes.” Also known as a Spirit Board, it was said that the dead were able to contact the living and reportedly used a talking board very similar to a modern Ouija board by Spiritualists and amateurs to enable communication with the spirit world.

A grandfather and his grandson, supervised by the family dog, cut pumpkins for jack o'lanterns. After their introduction by Irish immigrants to the United States in the mid-nineteenth century, the carving of jack o'lanterns from pumpkins began, as they were native to the region rather than the beets or turnips used in Ireland. The folklore about Stingy Jack and his tricking the devil was quickly incorporated into Halloween in Boston, and we've been carving pumpkins with happy, sad, and spooky faces ever since.

Mr. Macklin takes his knife
And carves the yellow pumpkin face
Three holes bring eyes and nose to life,
The mouth has thirteen teeth in place.
Then Mr. Macklin just for fun
Transfers the corn-cob pipe from his
Wry mouth to Jack's, and everyone
Dies laughing! O what fun it is
Till Mr. Macklin draws the shade
And lights the candle in Jack's skull.

David McCord

On the cover of the *Saturday Evening Post* on October 23, 1920, Norman Rockwell depicted a child covered in a white sheet holding a jack o'lantern on a stick and scaring her grandfather, who raises his hands in alarm. His glasses have fallen off his face, as well as spooking the family dog. The story of Stingy Jack, for whom the jack o'lantern was named, was a devious fellow who met the devil one fateful night. The duo shared a drink and, too cheap to pay for his booze, Jack convinced Satan to morph into a coin that he could use to pay for their beverages. As soon as he did, Jack put the coin in his pocket next to a silver cross. The devil was unable to change back into his original form, and Jack held him that way until Satan agreed not to take his soul.

Rust Craft Greeting Card Company was started in 1906 by Fred Winslow Rust in Kansas City, Missouri. Fred Rust was later joined by his brother, Donald Rust, and their greeting cards "always strove to maintain the highest standards in design, reproduction, and composition." Rust Craft revolutionized the use of the "French Fold," a method of folding paper into quarters in order to print a card on a single sheet of paper with a single printed side. Many of the "firsts" in the greeting card industry belong to Rust Craft, including anniversary and graduation cards. Fred Rust and his staff wrote many of the most popular messages. First located in Boston's South End, it moved in 1954 to Rustcraft Road in Dedham, Massachusetts. (Courtesy of the Maine State Library)

Rust Craft often had very colorful Halloween cards, both in design and sayings in the greeting. This card, "From One Old Bat ... " shows a cheerful winged bat on the card. However, we have no idea how the old bat who received the card took the Halloween greeting!

This Rust Craft Halloween card covers all the bases with a spooky quartet of a witch, a ghost, a skeleton, and a black cat with its back arched, peering over a wood fence.

Ghosts 'n Goblins by the batch
Just for Yooooooo to mix 'n match

An adorable black kitten, with huge eyes, stares out at us in a hat with a crescent moon and a spider as it emerges from a jack o'lantern. With bats flying about, the full Harvest moon bathes the card in light.

Black cats, witches' hats
Jack o'lanterns Jack o'lanterns
Black, orange, white, green
These are the colors of Halloween

Tasha Tudor, seen weaving dried flowers from her garden into a decorative autumnal wreath, was an author and artist whosc grccting cards evoke an old fashioned quality and the charm of home life. She was known across the country for her glowing watercolor depictions of the New England rural scene of a century ago and for her exquisite paintings of children, flowers, and animals. Born Starling Burgess, she was the daughter of naval architect W. Starling Burgess, known as "the Skipper," and noted portrait painter Rosamond Tudor.

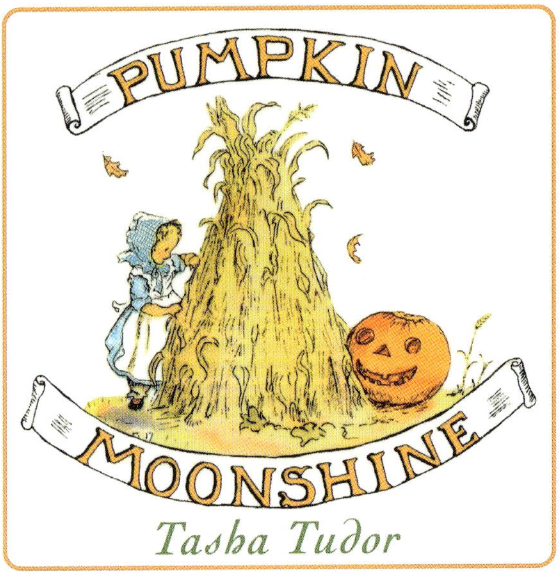

Pumpkin Moonshine was written by Tasha Tudor in 1938 and was her very first book in which she writes of celebrating fall and Halloween in all its glory. Tudor was known for her glowing watercolor depictions of the American rural scene of a century ago and for her exquisite paintings of children, flowers, and animals. In the book, it's almost Halloween, and little Sylvie Ann has found the biggest, fattest pumpkin in the patch! But before she can carve it into a giant, crooked-toothed pumpkin moonshine, or jack o'lantern, she has to get it hom—but it is so huge!

Ellen H. Clapsaddle was a noted artist and prolific creator of postcards at the turn of the twentieth century. Here she depicts two women, one of the seventeenth century wearing a witch's hat, holding a black cat with a small cauldron over her arm, and a fashionable woman of the early twentieth century in a satin gown, fur collar and muff, a feather bedecked hat, and holding a lorgnette.

For Hallowe'en
Old Style and New

Frances Isabelle Lockwood Brundage was a well-known and successful illustrator of children's classics such as the novels of Louisa May Alcott, Johanna Spyri, and Robert Louis Stevenson, and traditional literary collections such as *The Arabian Nights* and the stories of King Arthur and Robin Hood. She was a well-known illustrator for Louis Prang, whose factory in Boston produced high quality greeting cards. Wolff Hagelberg, one of Europe's leading fine art publishers, and Raphael Tuck, art publishers to Their Majesties King Edward and Queen Alexandra, produced valentines and postcards. Here she has a jovial witch in colorful garb with her broom under her arm and her black cat sitting on a crescent moon.

The clock is striking midnight
The witch her spell has cast
All fairies, ghosts and goblins
Will be conjured from the past

The Hallowe'en Lantern, commonly known as a jack o'lantern, is held by a woman dressed in black with a red cape. A screaming black cat and an intensely staring moon, along with its moon beams, bathes the scene in an eerie light.

At twelve o'clock you must be ready
And hold your pumpkin good and steady
For by its rays of candle light
On Hallowe'en all things are bright!

Hallowe'en Time shows a young girl sleeping as winged fairies hover over her, and goblins lurk at the top of her pillow. Fairies are a magical creature, including goblins and gnomes, and are said to symbolize a deep connection between living beings and nature, acting as mediators between plants, animals, and the various elements of nature.

Tonight, upon your pillow,
Close your eyes and hide your head,
For the fairies and the goblins
Will be hovering round your bed.

A young girl, depicted within a bat filled diamond, stands before an open fire upon which she has thrown the shells of two walnuts upon which she wrote two names. Originating with the ancient Celts, single women would designate a walnut for each of their love interests, then toss the nuts into a fire on Halloween. If the nut popped and jumped, her marriage would be filled with quarrels and strife. However, if the nuts burned peacefully side by side, that was the best omen for a future of no strife.

Write on the shells of two walnuts the names
Of two of your sweethearts and throw in the flames
The shell that cracks first is your lover's name
Be good to him and date he'll proclaim.

Nearing the stroke of midnight on Halloween night, this woman peers into a mirror while holding a candle in a jack o'lantern and discovers the face of her future husband. Other rituals include combing one's hair while staring into the mirror as well as cutting an apple into nine slices and eating them from a fruit knife, again standing in front of the mirror. It was not always successful, and some saw a skull reflected in the mirror, which sadly meant one would die before marrying.

If at midnight with a pumpkin light
You steal to your room unseen
In the mirror appears the face
Of your lover true on Hallowe'en

Here a woman peers into her mirror, which has always been thought of as portals to the shadow world, to hopefully see her future husband as her dastardly brother crouches in the doorway and holds a jack o'lantern aloft on a stick to thwart her effort.

If you are too anxious on Hallowe'en
To peep in the mirror before midnight
Instead of the face of your lover you seemingly
A big pumpkin head that's fancy free.

A Thrilling Hallowe'en! Ellen H. Clapsaddle depicts two frightened children reading *Ye Ghost Story.* Tis' certainly a thrilling Hallowe'en. Clapsaddle was a well-known artist at the turn of the twentieth century who is recognized as one of the most prolific postcard and greeting card artists of her era. Clapsaddle's greatest success was in the development of her artwork into single-faced cards that could be mailed as postcards.

Ellen H. Clapsaddle depicts *A Jolly Hallowe'en* and had a boy dressed in a white collared robe holding a large jack o'lantern; the boy's arm has a metal rivet that allows the arm and pumpkin to move to cover his face. Clapsaddle was acclaimed during her career for her prodigious work and her artistic designs have become highly prized; she is credited with over 3,000 designs in the postcard field during her career.

Tonight is the night when pumpkins stare
Through sheaves and leaves everywhere,
When ghoul and ghost and goblin host
Dance round their queen
It's Halloween.

Holding her dog close to her, this young girl passes a window with a spooky illuminated jack o'lantern peering inside. This card is a charm to keep you from harm this Hallowe'en.

Jack-o'-lanterns grinning, shadows on a screen,
Shrieks and starts and laughter--
This is Halloween!

This Hallowe'en card was printed by the George C. Whitney Company in 1910. The little girl, dressed as a pumpkin with pumpkin-puff sleeves and a pumpkin skirt, is surrounded by the wilds of the night including a mouse, black cat, owl, and raven illuminated by the moon. Even the tree on the left is in on the act pulling a face at the trembling girl.

Histi and Harki Draw close and tremble
'Tis this night that ghosts assemble!

Two black cats, one in a witch's hat with a baton and the other sporting an eye bandage, carry an unsmiling bass drum across a field as they are watched by field mice.

Fee, fo, fi, fum...
Two cats and a big bass drum
Here's hoping, Hallowe'en night,
You will get an awful fright...

A black cat acts as a maestro with a baton in his paw as he leads a group of singing jack o'lanterns in a musical piece as bats fly above.

Sing a song of Halloween
Pumpkins everywhere
Cats and bats and witches
are flying through the air

Hallowe'en Greetings was printed by George C. Whitney Company in 1918. Two jack o'lanterns, with lighted chamber candlesticks flanking them, smile sinisterly at one another as ghosts fly high above.

By yellow, mellow candle light,
While ghosts and goblins meet to-night,
I hope good luck will come your way
And stay with you for many a day

A coven, with their witch's hats and broom sticks, dancc around a hugc iron cauldron as others can be seen in the distance on their way to join them. Here on Halloween night witches gather under a full moon to make potions, cast spells, and have a jolly good time.

I send my Hallowe'en greetings this year
By seven old witches from far and from near
Weaving spells of good weather and spells of good cheer

Halloween Greeting: A witch in her black witch's hat, flowing cape, and colorful flowered dress, kneels to pat her black cat as an owl, other black cats, and jack o'lanterns look on. In witchcraft, one can wear white clothing when working with magic for purity or to bring about peace as it is used to signify spirituality, peace, and purity in many cultures.

Dame Fortune will have smiled on me
Her cats the blackest ever seen...
Will have brought to me the best of luck
If I may see you on Hallowe'en

8

A Beacon Hill Halloween

Dressed in their festive Halloween costumes, these bronze ducklings in the Public Garden in Boston were sculpted by Nancy Schon as a recreation of the mallard family in Robert McCloskey's children's classic book *Make Way for Ducklings*. Seen here, the ducklings, Jack, Kack, Lack, Mack, Nack, Ouack, Pack, and Quack, are led by Mrs. Mallard, who in the classic story lived on an island in the lagoon in the Boston Public Garden. Mrs. Mallard "taught them to walk in a line, to come when they were called, and to keep a safe distance from bikes and scooters and other things with wheels." They are on their way to visit policeman Michael, who feeds them peanuts daily. These bronze ducklings have become an icon of Boston.

18 Louisburg Square on Beacon Hill is eerily draped in spider cobwebs on the facade along with ghosts on the fence and staircase. Louisburg Square is one of two residential squares on Beacon Hill, Pemberton Square having been developed for a new court house beginning in 1885. Although Louisburg Square can boast no Bulfinch designed houses, as they were built between 1833 and 1847, and is much more modern than some other sections of Beacon Hill, its retiring charm and English flavor make it one of the most attractive features of the neighborhood, especially at Halloween.

Decorated with pumpkins and illuminated jack o'lanterns, Louisburg Square takes on a Halloween theme at dusk. The red brick swell bay facade Greek Revival houses around Louisburg Square, a park owned by the twenty-eight lot owners who signed the Proprietors Indenture and Articles of Agreement and which ensured current and subsequent homeowners would act as stewards of the shared land, is one of the icons of Boston. The Proprietors of Louisburg Square is considered the earliest example of a homeowner association in America. With lighted doorways, trick-or-treaters scamper from house to house.

Many residents of Beacon Hill create Halloween-themed decorations that delight as well as spook those on Halloween night. Here on Pinckney Street spider cobwebs have been strung from house shutters to a tree, creating an eerie arbor that children run under while out trick-or-treating.

29A Chestnut Street, on the left, was designed by Charles Bulfinch and built in 1800 as a side facing house with an Ionic columned entrance. Charles Bulfinch set out pattern streets, designed mansions, and created an elegant urbane setting on Beacon Hill, and this house was one of the first built. The house retains its side garden and the distinctive purple windowpanes and is decorated with witches, hanging ghosts, mummies, and skeletons, as well as faux slate headstones set in the garden to spook as well as delight.

A young boy dressed as Spider Man approaches a house on Chestnut Street on Beacon Hill with not one but two pumpkin buckets to hold his candy treats. Adults got into the Halloween theme by dressing as a pirate, vampire, and barmaid. Chestnut Street has three-story row houses that blended both nineteenth century architectural details with elegant embellishments such as demilune windows and sidelights at the front door, arched windows, and others that created an attractive neighborhood. Cornelius Coolidge designed the row houses from 48 to 60 Chestnut Street, seen on the left.

With mini electric pumpkin lights strung across the street, children might be spooked by the spider cobwebs that cover the windows and the tiny orange twinkly lights. Residents of Beacon Hill created Halloween themed decorations that were brilliant in the dark of the night.

Acorn Street is one of the most photographed streets in Boston, with its quaint row houses, brick sidewalks, and its narrow cobblestone paved street. Original cobblestone streets are now rare in Boston and considered historic treasures. A street paved with these multi-hued, variously shaped cobblestones retains its original character and charm, and can be quite beautiful, but dreadful to walk or drive on. Here, with its charming lanterns, the street is decorated for Halloween awaiting the swarms of children at dusk.

The theme for this homeowner's Halloween spectacle was Carnival, which is a season or festival of merrymaking! With striped awnings and a door entramement that was a larger-than-life mouth with mammoth teeth at the top of the opening and Carnival spelled out in blinking light bulbs, Halloween visitors could look at themselves in the trick mirrors before getting treats at the front door. Carnivals held under a big top awning often featured costume contests, trick-or-treating, and special Halloween versions of popular Carnival activities such as the trick mirrors that distorted one's appearance, a great way to skip the candy.

Nothing says Halloween more than skulls impaled on a cast iron fence with strings of electric lights composed of tibia and fibula bones. This was a gruesome display but certainly catches the attention of both children as well as adults. Skeletons are striking Halloween symbols because they are a stark reminder of death. Skeletons serve to remind us that Halloween has always been a holiday about the dead as All Hallows' Eve.

Halloween on Beacon Hill draws hundreds of costumed children who, with their parents and guardians, stroll through the streets admiring the interesting Halloween decorations while trick-or-treating for candy. Here, an orange and black balloon canopy and side balloon displays marks the entrance to Acorn Street.

It's late and we are sleepy, the air is cold and still.
Our jack-o-lantern grins at us upon the window sill.
We're stuffed with cake and candy and we've had a lot of fun,
But now it's time to go to bed and dream of all we've done.

Some homeowners really get into the groove of Halloween. A woman dressed as a witch in a huge witch's hat and black gown greets trick-or-treaters as they approach the doorway. 282 Marlborough Street is in the Back Bay of Boston and was designed by Ware and Van Brundt and built in 1872, and at one time served as the residence of the rector of St. Paul's Episcopal Cathedral on Tremont Street in Boston.

Seen at dusk on Halloween night, illuminated floating creatures envelope this row house at 235 Marlborough Street in Boston's Back Bay from top to bottom. A sea serpent slithers on the front garden and walkway with jellyfish or amoebas dangling from ropes along the facade. With blue and while colored lights, the marine life seems to come to life and literally acts as a beacon for Halloween revelers. The row house, one of four at 233-235-237-239 Marlborough Street were once owned by Eben D. Jordan and Charles Marsh, partners in the Jordan Marsh Department Store that began in Boston in 1851.

This row house had spooky ghosts suspended by ropes that swaying in the dark must have been a frightening sight for children. With a huge spider enveloped in a cobweb on the projecting oriole, as well as spider webs on the cast iron fence, stacks of pumpkins and ghostly apparitions all served to scare as well as delight even the most jaded celebrators of Halloween.

Enormous winged dinosaur balloons seem ready to swoop down on any trick-or-treaters brave enough to run the walkway to the front door of this house for candy! With the use of pulleys, these fearsome dragons could be raised and lowered to create panic in anyone who approached.

9

Halloween Cheesecake

Helen Bennett was a model often appearing in *Vogue* and was formerly Miss Missouri. She began her acting career in the late 1930s, appearing in films such as *The Middleton Family* at the New York World's Fair, *The Royal Mounted Rides Again*, *Because of Him*, *The Scarlet Horseman*, *Lost City of the Jungle*, *Francis in the Haunted House* and *Step Down to Terror*. She was also a popular television star, appearing on *The Donna Reed Show*, *Lux Video Theatre*, and *The Vice*. Her attention to style and grooming earned her recognition by Monsieur Leon, a prominent New York hairstylist who promoted the well-groomed "new look" in the late 1940s. Seen here, Miss Bennett is ethereally dressed in 1939 in a "Spider Dress," a chic black Halloween gown with a spiderweb silk over skirt.

Betty Grable, whose real name was Elizabeth Ruth Grable, was a popular actress in the 1940s and was said to be the highest-salaried woman in the United States in the mid-twentieth century. In 1939, Grable appeared opposite her then-husband Jackie Coogan in *Million Dollar Legs*, a comedy that gave Grable her famous nickname. In fact, she was photographed by Frank Powolny in 1942 posing in a tight, one-piece bathing suit and became an instant pinup icon with the soldiers and sailors serving during World War II. Grable's many films during the 1930s and 1940s grossed more than $100 million, and for ten consecutive years she reigned in the Quigley poll's top ten box office stars. She is seen here reading *Halloween and Spook Stories*, flashing her million-dollar legs.

Cyd Charise, whose real name was Tula Ellice Finklea, fetchingly poses in her witch's hat and corn broom in front of a trio of pumpkins. Among her most popular movies were those that featured her dancing such as *Singin' in the Rain, The Band Wagon, Brigadoon* with Gene Kelly and Van Johnson, and *Silk Stockings*. In the movie *The Band Wagon*, where she danced with Astaire, the critic Pauline Kael said that "when the bespangled Charisse wraps her phenomenal legs around Astaire, she can be forgiven everything, even her three minutes of 'classical' ballet and the fact that she reads her lines as if she learned them phonetically." Charise was featured in the *Guinness Book of World Records* under "Most Valuable Legs" because a $5 million insurance policy was reportedly issued on her legs in 1952.

Adle Jergens, whose real name was Adele Louisa Jurgenson, was aptly named "Miss World's Fairest" at the 1939 New York World's Fair. In the early 1940s, she danced as a Radio City Rockette and was named the Number One Showgirl in New York City. After such popular fame she went on to become an understudy to Gypsy Rose Lee in the Broadway show *Star and Garter* in 1942. Jergens landed a coveted movie contract with Columbia Pictures in 1944, which precluded that she become a blond. Here in a two-piece bikini with long fingerless gloves and a black plumed witch's hat, she poses with her newly blond tresses between a jack o'lantern and an arched black cat shadow.

Paulette Goddard, whose real name was Marion Levy, began her career as a child fashion model and went on to become a performer in several Broadway productions as a Ziegfeld Girl. However, Charlie Chaplin, whom she married, tutored Goddard in the art of acting, and he displayed the results in his final silent film, *Modern Times*, in which Goddard portrayed the Gamine, an effervescent female companion to Chaplin's famous character Little Tramp. With Bob Hope, she starred in *The Cat and the Canary*, *The Ghost Breakers*, and *Nothing but the Truth*; she was part of the all-female cast of *The Women* and she starred in *Hold Back the Dawn*. Seen here in a kitten cloche hat and whiskers holding a jack o'lantern, a reprise of her movie *The Cat and the Canary*, she looks pensive with a silhouette of her as a cat starring at a caged canary.

Anne Nagel, whose real name was Anna Marie Dolan, was enrolled as a child by her parents at Notre Dame Academy in Boston, with the expectation she would become a nun. She quickly outgrew this expectation and secured a part as a ballet girl in *Hypnotized*, her "first documented feature credit." She was one of fourteen young women "launched on the trail of film stardom" in 1935, when they each received a six-month contract with 20th Century Fox after spending eighteen months in the company's training school. In 1940, she appeared with W. C. Fields and Mae West in *My Little Chickadee* as well *as Black Friday*, *Hot Steel*, and *Diamond Frontiers*. She also appeared on the radio in the role of Miss Case in The Green Hornet *radio series,* a role she reprised for both of the filmed serials *The Green Hornet* and *The Green Hornet Strikes Again!* Here she sits on a larger-than-life jack o'lantern with her broom at the ready.

Barbara Bates was a well-known singer and actress. She appeared with some of the biggest stars of the day including Bette Davis in *June Bride* and Danny Kaye in *The Inspector General*. Her success in these movies led to her auditioning for the role of Phoebe in Fox's upcoming movie *All About Eve*. In competition for the part was Zsa Zsa Gabor, but Bates impressed the producers and was given the part. She made a short but important appearance as the devious schemer, Phoebe, at the end of the film. Bates's image is enshrined in the film's last scene, posing in front of a three-way mirror, while holding the award won by her idol Eve Harrington, played by Anne Baxter. Later, she co-starred in *Cheaper by the Dozen*, and its sequel *Bells on Their Toes*, with Jeanne Crain and Myrna Loy. Seen here in a satin bikini, fur mittens, and cat ears, she stares at a jack o'lantern in a shock of hay as a black cat prowls on the left.

Lillian Wells began her career as a model and it led to parts in the movies *Dead Reckoning, Down to Earth,* and *Framed*. Though she appeared in a half dozen movies, she never became a well-known actress and eventually returned to modeling. Here, dressed in a Harlequin blouse and black shorts, she kneels in an eerie photograph of a picket fence and arched-back cat in shadows framed by shocks of corn.

From left to right are Barbara Britton, Katherine Booth, Ella Neal, and Eva Gabor. Each of these beautiful witches has a corn broom along with their witch's hats. Although broomsticks are said to serve various magical purposes, and provided a means of transportation, their main use was for clearing away negative energy ahead of a ritual. Here in front of a picket fence surmounted by a black arch-backed cat, they caution us to be quiet before they begin their magic ritual.

Ann Miller, whose real name was Johnnie Lucille Collier, was a noted singer and dancer, who was famous for her incredible speed in tap dancing, once claiming she could tap 500 times per minute. An elegant and statuesque actress, she is best remembered for her work in the classic Hollywood cinema musicals of the 1940s and 1950s and she starred in the movie musical classics such as Vincent Minnelli's *Easter Parade*, Stanley Donen's *On the Town*, and George Sidney's *Kiss Me Kate*. Miller has a well-earned star on the Hollywood Walk of Fame. Here in a striped jersey and shorts, she holds a star bedecked witch's hat and is surrounded by black cat faces and a trio of jack o'lanterns.

Veronica Lake, whose real name was Constance Frances Marie Ockelman, was best known for her *femme fatale* roles in film noirs with Alan Ladd during the 1940s and her signature peek-a-boo hairstyle of long blonde tresses. Among her many movies were *I Wanted Wings*, *Sullivan's Travels*, *The Blue Dahlia*, and aptly as a seventeenth-century sorceress who falls for the ancestor of the man who condemned her to death in Rene Clair's *I Married A Witch*. Seen here in her veiled witch's hat and broom, surrounded by cauldrons and jack o'lanterns, she posed in a reprise of her performance in the "bizarre but beguiling" sorceress in *I Married A Witch*.

Ann Savage, whose real name was Berniece Maxine Lyon, was a popular film and television actress. She is best remembered as the cigarette-puffing *femme fatale* in the critically acclaimed film noir *Detour*. It was said that she achieved major cult stardom with her hard-bitten blonde looks and "Perfect Vixen" tag. Ann Savage in real life was a lovely, spirited, gentle-looking lady; she was one of the more popular WWII pinups. After appearing in a photo layout in *Esquire* magazine in 1944, she became a favorite performer with the troops, making numerous personal appearance tours at various military bases in order to raise money for war bonds. Miss Savage is seen in her witch's hat and fishnet stockings perched on a pneumatic harpoon gun.

Martha Vickers, whose real name was Martha MacVicar, began her career as a model and cover girl and during World War II and was a popular pinup girl in *Yank, the Army Weekly*. Though she had small parts in movies such as *Frankenstein Meets the Wolf Man* and *The Mummy's Ghost*, she would star in *The Big Sleep*, with Humphrey Bogart, playing the teenage nymphet "bad girl" for all it was worth, *The Time, the Place and the Girl* and the film noir *The Man I Love* with Ida Lupino, and finally earned leading lady status in *That Way with Women* opposite Dane Clark. She appeared in the melodrama *Bad Boy*, which was Audie Murphy's first starring role. Seen here, Miss Vickers is dressed in a black-and-white two piece with a witch's hat as she stirs the bubbling cauldron with a long wooden spoon.

Gale Robbins, born Betty Gale Murphy, was described in the newspaper as "the famous model whose face has appeared on the covers of many leading magazines, and whose eyes and teeth are the trademarks respectively of Murine and Iodent." A well-known singer, in 1949 she sang as part of Dennis Day's *Vaudeville* show in Boston, prompting a reviewer for the trade publication *Billboard* to write: "The acts include Gale Robbins, as fine a vocalist as the town has seen in ages. She's pretty, has a real voice and a personality which never flags." During World War II, Gale was featured on the cover of *Yank, the Army Weekly*, was heard on radio, and toured with Bob Hope in Europe entertaining the troops. Among her movies were *Race Street, The Barcleys of Broadway, Three Little Words, The Fuller Brush Girl,* and *Calamity Jane*. Here, in an apple tipped witch's hat, she cuddles up to a pipe smoking scarecrow.

Gloria Saunders, whose real name was Gloria Ella Saunders, started her career as a child working in the radio industry. She would later have recurring roles in two of the earliest television series being cast in the role of Ah Toy in *Mysteries in Chinatown*. Later she appeared in five episodes of another syndicated western series *The Range Rider*. Her success led to her appearance in the movies *Terry the Pirates, Red Snow*, and *Cry Danger*. Seen here, grasping a pumpkin under one arm, she catches her dress on barbed wire as she glances back apprehensively at a scarecrow looming above her.